Dynamics
of
Catholic Education

••••••

Letting the Catholic School Be School

••••••

Louis DeThomasis, FSC, PhD

PUBLICATIONS

DEDICATION

To Saint John Baptist De LaSalle and his Brothers,
as Jesus lives in their hearts forever!

DYNAMICS OF CATHOLIC EDUCATION
Letting the Catholic School Be School
by Louis DeThomasis, FSC, PhD

Edited by Gregory F. Augustine Pierce
Cover design by Tom A. Wright
Interior design and typesetting by Patricia A. Lynch

Copyright © 2013 by Louis DeThomasis

Published by ACTA Publications, 4848 N. Clark Street, Chicago, IL 60640,
(800) 397-2282, www.actapublications.com

An earlier version of this book titled *Beyond the Story* was published by Garratt Publishing in
Australia in 2012.

Library of Congress Catalog Number: 2013940352
ISBN: 978-0-87946-511-7
Printed in the United States of America by Total Printing Systems
Year 20 19 18 17 16 15 14 13
Printing 12 1110 9 8 7 6 5 4 3 2 First
♻ Text printed on 30% post-consumer recycled paper

CONTENTS

PART TWO
DYNAMICS NEEDED FOR THE
TRANSFORMATION OF CATHOLIC SCHOOLS

INTRODUCTION

• • • • • •

Jesus of Nazareth could have chosen simply to express himself in moral precepts; but like a great poet he chose the form of the parable, wonderful short stories that entertained and clothed the moral precept in an eternal form. It is not sufficient to catch man's mind, you must also catch the imaginative faculties of his mind.

DUDLEY NICHOLS

• • • • • •

As I did in my book, *Flying in the Face of Tradition—Listening to the Lived Experience of the Faithful* (2012), I have attempted to make this work more approachable and readable to a wider audience; therefore, I do not approach the subject matter with a formalized, academic-research structure. In that book, I presented my conviction that a quandary exists in today's institutional Catholic Church. At the core of this quandary is the institutional church's reluctance to embrace the idea of tradition as a source of divine revelation obtained by effectively listening to and learning from the lived experience of the faithful followers of Jesus Christ.

Without diminishing the church's formal teaching authority, i.e. the *magisterium*, Catholic tradition unfolds over time—and continues to unfold—as the followers of Jesus of Nazareth also contribute their insights of Holy Scripture and especially the sacred stories within the Old and New Testaments based on their lived experiences and the culture that surrounds them. This is called the *sensus fidelium* or sense of the faithful. Tradition is the dynamic that propels the story of the response to Jesus throughout the two millennia since the Word came into the world. Or, as it was eloquently said by the Prefect of the Congregation of the Doctrine of the Faith, Archbishop Gerhard Muller, that the development of a culture of communion implies "…that equal attention be given to communion with the bishops of the Church, communion with the local dioceses and parishes, communion with the Catholic faithful, and the bonds of charity and friendship with those still separated from the Church."

The powerful gospel story of Peter as the Rock upon which the church is built is considered a true and timeless justification for the institutional structures that have evolved over the centuries. Indeed, that compelling sacred story and image have been the explanation that the institutional church embraces to justify the transitions and paradigm shifts that have emerged. However, some ambiguity exists with this image. Does the lived experience of the faithful today tell us that when what I call here "the institutional church" speaks, listeners are hearing the voice of Peter, the Rock, on which the church stands; or are we hearing the voice of the church on which Peter, the Rock, stands? There is ambiguity when we try to clearly answer the "who, what, where, and why" of how tradition as a source of revelation works today. Some of us in the church are still seeking clarification, while others see this as a blessed ambiguity needing no answer, because *Roma locuta est, Causa finita est!* (Rome has spoken. The question is closed!)

······

A growing number of us who have been faithful all our lives are having difficulty recognizing the institutional church as the Rock that Jesus established.

······

In today's world, however, because the actions of the institutional church are reported immediately throughout the globe, there are very few secrets that actually stay secrets. Likewise, there are very few questions that are closed just because Rome says so. The undeniable fact is that there is a growing number of us who have been faithful all our lives and are having difficulty recognizing the institutional church as the Rock that Jesus established. Rather they now experience these "man-made" organizational structures (and I do mean *man* made) as a departure from what Jesus had in mind. We fail to see Christ in many of the directives and pronouncements coming out of Rome.

In essence, the question I am asking is this: Are today's actions of the institutional church, not its words or pietistic exhortations making us a church of *communio* (that we may all be one) as Jesus established with Peter; or are its actions making us a church where we all must be the same by excluding those who differ with or question the Rock?

Seeking oneness through inclusion rather than exclusion is the tradition I was taught, the one that is so clearly unfolded by the sacred stories in Holy Scripture. Based on this realization, I observed in *Flying in the Face of Tradition*:

> Sexual abuse, corruption, authoritarianism, lack of transparency, and cover-ups have all been collapsing into and on top of the institutional church. It does not matter whether one is liberal or conservative, orthodox or unorthodox, believer or non-believer. One cannot help but be amazed that the prestige, reverence, and esteem that once belonged to the institutional church and its leaders are no longer there. The tipping point has been reached, and the moral authority, honor, and respect that the institutional church once elicited from most peoples and secular institutions around the globe simply no longer exist.

If we do not unravel the quandary that has been caused by the institutional church's own actions, the resulting negative stories exploding all over the world, coupled with the institutional church's restrictive imposition on open dialogue among the faithful, will cause the church to continue to be mired and steeped in division. The successor to Peter once again must be seen standing firmly as the Rock—not with a distorted view of tradition that calls for re-creating some nostalgic past but rather with a dynamic, grace-filled, and Holy Spirit-inspired living tradition that creates a new future for the People of God in the new globalized world. The core truth found in the sacred story of the Rock is not Peter seeking to control reality by issuing doctrines, dogma, and dictums. It is a tradition of preaching the Gospel of Jesus Christ in an engaging, transparent, candid, and open dialogue to the emerging People of God so that we may freely respond to Christ's message of love. Peter, the Rock, brought the freedom, forgiveness, acceptance, and love of Jesus Christ to the people of the world. He did not try to bring the people of the world into a regal and rigid institution!

An abiding love and respect for the church and its *magisterium* (teaching authority) can be realized only if the Rock upon which the faithful stand today is the same Rock that Jesus gave to us in Peter: the Rock that helps create our future, not duplicate our past; the Rock that is an invitation to an abundant life, not the caretaker of historical details and artifacts; the Rock that acts out of love and sensitivity, not dictums and threats of excommunication. It is in the spirit of tradition, properly understood, that the Holy Spirit creates the church of the People of God. It is that tradition, properly understood, that will rescue the church from its current quandary and transform it into the loving servant it was called to be from the initial call to Peter.

In Part One, *Letting the Catholic School Be School*, I present a case for the role of Catholic education as a major source to help the church reestablish its relevance and vitality, becoming the exemplar of a spiritual dynamic that is so needed in our new, globalized world. I believe it is a very realistic possibility that Catholic education can respond to our need for transformation because it has always responded with great effectiveness and dedication to the needs of the church and the world alike.

I will explore the future of Catholic education, going down two paths at once: how Catholic education can help the church begin to unravel the difficult quandary it has gotten itself into and how it can help the church improve its relationship with its own members and the world at large.

Although this overview presents a case for the role of Catholic education in general, it will be obvious that there is a distinct focus on Catholic higher education, which is where I spent much of my career. Even with this slant toward higher education, however, my hope is that the basic principles—with adaptations—could be applied pedagogically, in appropriate and relevant ways, at all levels of Catholic educational institutions.

There is a persistent and valid question asked today by many dedicated Catholic educators: Will the institutional church cooperate in this effort at transformation and let Catholic schools really be schools rather than propaganda venues? Significant pressures, criticisms, and intrusions from Catholic conservative and even fundamentalist ideologues within the church have caused much turmoil and anxiety among many Catholic educators and their institutions. However, the twin graces of zeal and faith at the core of Catholic education are dynamic enough to lead the People of God and all people of good will beyond their nostalgic beliefs. These two core graces are at the heart and soul of Catholic education. They are how relationships are born and flourish as the hallmark of a distinct and unique approach to Catholic education around the world.

To accomplish its mission, Catholic education must continue with courageous, dynamic, and effective initiatives. It must ensure that it remains a vital and relevant force for good in the third millennium. If it does this, it will continue to be vibrant and relevant in today's world, which is in desperate need of a practical witness to Christ's unconditional love. But the institutional church must permit the Catholic education system to truly educate and not just catechize. It must let the Catholic school really be school!

• • • • • •

The institutional church must permit the Catholic education system to truly educate and not just catechize.

• • • • • •

In Part Two, *Dynamics Needed for the Transformation of Catholic Schools*, I explore ingredients that are needed in order to transform any institution in today's globalized society. For intentional transformation to take place, specific and effective dynamics and qualities must be utilized in order to accomplish a new and vital existence for an institution. These basic and foundational assumptions must first be identified and then incorporated into the culture of all institutions—Catholic schools and the Catholic Church included.

Transformation is always difficult, and there will always be those who resist efforts to do things differently. However, in a world that is so different from the past, it is important for all of us to understand the basic qualities needed for an institution to be responsive to the world that exists in the here and now. It is my hope that the Catholic Church, which cherishes so dearly its beautiful, rich traditions, will begin to live in the new emerging world and invent a future that will make the Gospel come alive again now. Catholic education can make that dream happen.

That leads me to a final note. Throughout the book I refer to "the church" or "the Catholic Church" and use the two terms pretty much interchangeably. Specifically I am referring to the Roman Catholic Church, of which I am a lifelong, faithful member. I am a Catholic school teacher and administrator, an educational consultant, a trustee to various Catholic organizations, and a De LaSalle Christian Brother for over forty years. I am not a theologian. So, I write this book as a committed and engaged Catholic educator using reasoned and informed Christian coomon sense—which is another word for tradition, properly understood.

As I started to work my way through the quandary the church is facing and how to unravel it, I constantly kept in mind and heeded advice from—of all people—that wonderful comedian, Gracie Allen, who said, "Don't place a period where God has placed a comma. God is still speaking."

So I begin now and try to write this book with as many commas and as few periods as possible.

Part One

......

Letting the Catholic School Be School

......

CHAPTER ONE

The Catholic School and Its Critics

· · · · · ·

I know no safe depository of the ultimate powers of the society but the people themselves; and if we think them not enlightened enough to exercise their control with a wholesome discretion, the remedy is not to take it from them, but to inform their discretion by education.

THOMAS JEFFERSON

· · · · · ·

Imagine a time traveler from today's globalized society going back to the day that Moses came down from the Mount with the Ten Commandments. As he stands next to the golden calf and hears the people complaining about the long list of commandments, you can hear him shout, "Hey you guys, if you think these Ten Commandments etched on two stone tablets have too many 'do's and don'ts', be thankful I didn't come down with a couple of MP3s!" Indeed, it would take at least a couple of hard drives with many gigabytes of storage for Catholic education to save all the advice from different constituencies telling them what they must do to be "Catholic." And not even Bill Gates could develop a computer program that would reconcile the various and competing expectations of Catholic education from so many well-intentioned people and produce a reasonable mission statement that would be accepted by everyone.

In this minefield of strongly competing forces and opinions, Catholic education should not try to walk a tight-rope in its attempt to balance its role as an educational institution and its responsibility to the Gospel. Religious fundamentalists, religious relativists, a few bishops, or ideologues of all stripes (who are often the loudest voices) should not be permitted to push the schools in one direction or the other.

Here is the main point of this book, and if you read no further at least take this away: The Catholic school must serve its students first. That may seem obvious, and it certainly is open to interpretation, but it is a truth that cannot be forgotten. For if a Catholic school does not serve its students first, it fails by definition. A school is not a church. May I repeat that? A school is not a church. It will not benefit those entrusted to its care—nor will it help the institutional church unravel its present quandary—if Catholic education does not provide a liberating intellectual education and an experience of human and religious development for its students.

* * * * * *

No amount of rote learning or access to digitally stored information is sufficient to illuminate and resolve the new emerging issues confronting students in today's globalized society.

* * * * * *

No amount of rote learning or access to digitally stored information is sufficient to illuminate and resolve the new emerging issues confronting students in today's globalized society. Our young people are confronted with a multitude of social and religious questions; some of the most pressing concern abortion and birth control; how to effectively employ a "preferential option for the poor;" relating new scientific knowledge about human sexuality to traditional church teachings; exploring ethical implications of human DNA engineering and manipulation of human genetic composition; embracing the concerns of women and men who, in growing numbers, feel abandoned by the institutional church; and so much more.

These issues and many additional and complex situations can be addressed by Catholic education only to the degree that schools are permitted to discuss them in an open and free environment. This is a vital concern for Catholic schools and strikes at the very heart of what it means to be a Catholic school. Consider a very real and specific contemporary situation that demonstrates this point.

Youngsters in primary, secondary, or university levels, who are developing as persons, may experience significant sexual uncertainties among their many other developmental dynamics, causing much confusion in their psychological journey to maturity. In this confusing period, some are confronted with internal psychological and hormonal episodes that psychologists tell us lead adolescent youngsters to be temporarily unsure of their sexuality. It is not uncommon that some may experience what they perceive as homosexual tendencies. They simply don't understand what is going on within their own developing body.

This is a time in young peoples' lives when they desperately need support and compassion from the church, the school, and their families, including sound professional and educational assistance. Yet, when they turn to the teachings of the institutional church, the official answer is that homosexuality is "disordered" and to act out of this disorder is seriously sinful. They are also told that love between two people of the same sex is condemned in Holy Scripture and that they can never get married or have a sexual relationship. No matter how much those in the institutional church may then use some intellectual gyrations and carefully nuanced distinctions about hating the sin and not the sinner, and no matter how much they contend they know everything there is to know about adolescent sexual development, nevertheless the young distraught persons only hear that they are condemned and disordered.

Making matters worse, those same youngsters are often terrified to openly discuss this question with their parents, and they certainly are not going anywhere near a church they feel is condemning them to hell for being a disordered human being! Let it be clearly said without any qualification, equivocation, or theological gyration: In a Catholic school at any level, these youngsters—in fact any confused or distressed young person—should find Jesus' *unconditional* love, support, understanding, solace, and relief. Nothing less!

All too often, and in growing numbers, there are young people with many real personal moral conflicts who feel isolated and abandoned by the church. If only the institutional church leaders relied more on Catholic educators to assist them in such situations, they could develop a more useful and profoundly human way to address these issues. My criticism is not a negative observation of the moral principle involved; rather it is a criticism of the growing perception that some in the institutional church are more concerned with the cold dogma than with the warm body hearing it. If people on both sides of the ideological spectrum would simply stop policing the Catholic schools and trust them to be truly Catholic by letting them do their jobs in a sensitive and correct pedagogical manner, there would be more healthy psychological support for young people who could be drawn to the church instead of abandoning it.

Catholic education can be a significant help to the church if it is able to resist the inappropriate infringement of its mission by the forces that see orthodoxy in terms of rigid formulistic statements of truth rather than the inclusive and holistic spirit of Christian love. Perhaps this current state of interaction between the Catholic school and the institutional church is similar to the situation of the nineteenth century short story writer, Guy de Maupassant: It was said of him that he ate his lunch each day at the restaurant on top of the Eiffel Tower because it was the only restaurant in Paris where he could eat without having to look at what he considered an architectural monstrosity!

Likewise, it seems that, because of the institutional church's increasing attempt to control its own people, the Catholic school is being forced to retreat into its own intellectual tower so it does not have to look on the ugliness of outside ideological and fundamentalist forces within its own church.

Catholic educators regularly experience complex and intricate forces that infringe on their identity. However, as long as they remain in their Eiffel Tower and turn a blind eye to what is happening to their schools, their future is unsure and unimpressive.

Catholic educators must be open to transformating themselves in order to respond to the very different needs of their students. They must have the courage to lead both the institutional church and all the People of God on the path to being a faithful Catholic, while at the same time running an excellent school. Catholic schools must guard against a conscious twisting of the truth in order to satisfy and keep peace with the growing intrusions in their pedagogical duties: what books are permitted, who should speak at the school, which teachers to hire or let go. How to relate the Catholic faith in conformity with the *magisterium* while embracing the rich and varied Catholic intellectual traditions is the responsibility of Catholic schools, not the institutional church. In essence, Catholic educators cannot bend to the demands of what their critics consider orthodoxy in order to keep peace. Of course Catholic schools have the responsibility to teach the Catholic faith accurately and responsibly. However, they are not to become automatons that are controlled by the click of a key from the institutional church's mainframe!

Catholic schools freely choose to be Catholic and, therefore, must be trusted to meet modern professional educational standards while concurrently unfolding the Catholic faith in ways that can produce understanding in world cultures of the third millennium. In this light, the Catholic school must walk a different and more treacherous tight-rope than the institutional church. After all, the institutional church is charged with proclaiming the Gospel to all by presenting its story using Scripture and tradition, while the Catholic school must take students beyond the story into the world. If we take a good look at the world today, there is no safety net under the Catholic schools walking that tight-rope as they try to accommodate their students, parents, faculties, benefactors, public accrediting agencies, the institutional church, and the ever-present orthodoxy police. Quite a formidable task!

• • • • • •

If the Catholic school tries to please everyone and be all things to all people, it will not be a school nor will it be Catholic.

• • • • • •

If the Catholic school tries to please everyone and be all things to all people, it will not be a school nor will it be Catholic. Such conscious circling around the truth and attempting to be all things to all people is not something peculiar at this moment in the history of the church. Consider for instance Tycho Brahe, a sixteenth-century Danish mathematician–philosopher, who "manufactured" a solution to Copernicus' then most distasteful (for the institutional church at the time) revelation that the Earth was not the center of the universe. Brahe made Copernicus' discovery much more palatable to the institutional church by agreeing that, indeed, all the planets revolved around the sun, just as Copernicus said. But, said Brahe, all those planets and the sun revolved around the Earth! What a pleasant intellectual and nuanced gyration, satisfying the institutional church with such a logical fabrication while, of course, simultaneously obfuscating the truth. Ah, but alas, all were then pleased with this intellectually rigorous (but truly tacky and ultimately untruthful) line of reasoning.

Throughout history, patterns of rationalizations manifest how people and institutions consciously work around the truth. Even in the history of the institutional church one can observe many partners in a dance of standard assumptions, phrases, actions, euphemisms, and hidden agendas. Procrustes, the robber in Greek mythology, cut people up to fit in his bed. Catholic educators today also live in a Procrustean world that they must resist. If they do not, then they will eventually be cut up and molded by the institutional church or the orthodoxy police to be something other than free, faithful, and relevant Catholic educators. They need to remember that a Catholic school is not the Catholic Church.

In no way should this warning be interpreted as a recommendation that the Catholic school should ignore the teaching authority of the church through its *magisterium*. The Catholic school has the obligation to present in a full and authentic way the teachings of the church. In my entire career as a Catholic educator, I was able to accomplish this goal. What I am saying is that the institutional church should stand clear of the Catholic school and trust the Catholic school to be Catholic. There is nothing wrong with encouraging helpful dialogue and candid discussion between the Catholic school and the institutional church. There is something very wrong, though, if the institutional church attempts to control the Catholic school and tries to cut it up and mold it to fit some preconceived, ideological form of the Catholic Church.

There has been much shouting directed against the Catholic school as it attempts to do its job of teaching as Jesus did. There is criticism when a Catholic school honors someone who deserves to be acknowledged if that honoree holds any single position that the critics believe to be against church orthodoxy— even if the honoree is not Catholic! There is likewise criticism from the official institutional church when theological research or speculation questions traditional church teachings in light of new knowledge that has been discovered, especially if it involves human sexuality. There are even religious ideologues from inside and from outside the church that criticize the Catholic school when it makes the distinction that there is necessarily a difference between the public's civil law and religious moral practice in a democratic society.

For example, a Catholic school should inform its students of the current position of the church that marriage is between a man and a woman. However, students should also be informed of the rationale from the opposite position as expounded in the realm of civil society if they are to be truly educated on the issues and the culture in which they live.

Ideological critics of Catholic schools certainly make their indignation known in a public way. The late Senator Huey Long once wrote in the margin of a speech that he was presenting, "Weak point, shout!" Catholic schools must not be intimidated by the decibel rating of the criticism. As a Catholic school interacts with the church, its students, and the culture it operates in, there will always be a multiplicity of considerations. And, usually, those shouting the loudest are the ones who deify their notion of correctness to the exclusion of any other reasonable voice on a particular topic. When any side in a controversy seeks to expand its moral force beyond logical constraints, it results in frightening and forced polarities. Perhaps more accurately such people should be described as the lunatic fringe!

Challenging such polarities unleashes great consternation and indignation that continues to hide the truth. Then the label throwing begins: "liberal," "conservative," "orthodox," "unorthodox," "faithful," "unfaithful," or—ultimately—"heretic." This label throwing does accomplish one thing—it divides people and thereby prevents them from coming together in celebration of Jesus' love.

When these combatant labels begin to be used, then all sides put on encumbering blinders that tarnish both the Catholic faith and its spirit of communion. The pit of ideology into which groups fall makes it as impossible for us to see reality as it was for de Maupassant to see the Eiffel Tower as he sat and ate his lunch atop the very tower he was avoiding. The results of such unproductive clashes are contrived and false. The Catholic school must identify itself to all as a true community of learners seeking information, knowledge, truth, and wisdom. In such a community there can be no prohibition or curtailment of inquiry that would inhibit the truly free and reasonable academic pursuit of knowledge and understanding. No interest group—not even the pope and the bishops—should encumber responsible academic freedom.

The Catholic school must be free to be a school so that it can truly educate a person seeking meaningfulness in a world of competing religions, philosophies, and values. The Catholic school conducts this search for truth within a commitment and dedication to the Catholic expression of faith, values, and teachings. There is an inestimable qualitative dimension created when the word "Catholic" is placed before "school." In essence the duty is established to bring the enlightenment of the Christian expression of faith and revelation to the noble pursuit of seeking truth and knowledge. And all must remember that faith is a gift from God and can be expressed in many different ways.

CHAPTER TWO

A Catholic School Is Not the Catholic Church, and the Catholic Church Is Not a Catholic School

••••••

As Catholics, we need not fall prey to the unfortunate but common notion that faith and science are incompatible, precisely because we believe that God is the Creator of all things... We can boldly seek to expand our knowledge of the empirical universe, assured that any truth we find through such avenues will not contradict the divinely revealed truths of our faith since all natural and supernatural truth comes from the same Creator.

REBECCA OAS, PHD

••••••

From the outset, it is important to state that the position taken here is that the Catholic school is (and must be) Catholic, but it is not (and must never be confused with) the church. In other words, Catholic education will be able to be an effective force in helping the church to actualize its mission to the degree that it is about education and schooling, not proselytizing and apologetics. Of course, these statements may seem counterintuitive and need to be explored and judged regarding their accuracy.

The first thing that needs to be said is that in no way do I mean to imply that Catholic education is vested with any special, magisterial powers or sacred foundations—these are attributable to the church and the church alone. The Catholic school cannot just make up what it thinks is the Catholic message. It can only teach it. A Catholic school is not the church and, as paradoxical as it may seem, that is why the future viability of the church, in order to be understood by the new generations of globalized people, is intimately connected with the future of Catholic education.

Jesus Christ said to St. Peter (Matthew 16: 18-19) that he is the Rock, the foundation of the church. In essence, Peter was then vested with the sacred mandate to teach, i.e. the power "to bind" and "to loose." There is no suggestion that Peter was to carry out this holy mission as the first President of a Catholic university or principal of the first Catholic primary or secondary school! The sacred and mysterious holiness of the church is to be church. As such, the Pope is teacher with a *magisterium*, a deposit of teachings, that interprets and preserves what has been revealed in Sacred Scripture and Tradition, the two sources of revelation recognized by the church. (For my thoughts on this important issue, see my previous book, *Flying in the Face of Tradition: Listening to the Lived Experience of the Church*.)

To this day, there is no historical example in the church, nor is there any serious theological conjecture I know of, that postulates that the teaching authority of the church is to be carried out by a school. I want to state unequivocally that the teaching authority of the church is vested in the church itself, not in any of its ministries, including that of education.

So where does this situation place Catholic education in its relationship to the church?

A careful and candid review (not often accomplished by ideologically fundamentalist-focused Catholics) of a document on Catholic colleges and universities by Pope John Paul II demonstrates the premise that Catholic schools are not the Catholic Church. It should be made clear that this document was written explicitly to Catholic higher education institutions, though there may be some extrapolation to primary and secondary Catholic schools. This document was promulgated on August 5, 1990, and takes its Latin name, *Ex Corde Ecclesiae,* from the first words of the document: "Born from the heart of the church."

At the very outset, Pope John Paul II makes it clear that the Catholic school, though related to the church, is not the church. The Catholic school had to be "born" from the heart of the church with "…institutional autonomy necessary to perform its functions effectively…" (12). And further clarifying this very important premise, the pope goes on to say that an essential characteristic of Catholic education is that there is to be "...a Christian inspiration not only of individuals but of the university community as such..." (13.1), thus recognizing, at least implicitly, that a Catholic school is outside the church and therefore needs its inspiration.

This institutional autonomy should not be something contentious or ambiguous in regard to understanding the identity of the Catholic school. The church recognizes this independence from the church as a necessity in order for the Catholic university to function effectively. Pope John Paul II would not have had to highlight this type of assurance if the Catholic school was a constitutive entity within the church. Instead, from its inception, the Catholic university was "born from the heart of the Church" and individuals and its community of educators freely accept inspiration from the church while the school maintains its autonomy from the church.

• • • • • •

A Catholic school is not an antagonist of the church, but it is necessarily separate from the church.

• • • • • •

Continuing his declaration of essential characteristics, Pope John Paul explicitly states that the Catholic university's commitment is to "... the service of the People of God and of the human family..." (12.4). He emphasizes that its responsibility is "...to consecrate itself without reserve to the cause of truth" (4). And that this should be accomplished "...in the context of the impartial search for truth that the relationship between faith and reason is brought to light and meaning" (5).

Such an impartial search for truth explicitly sets the Catholic educational mission. A Catholic school is not an antagonist of the church, but it is necessarily separate from the church. It cannot be impartial in its mission to the truth if the church controls its pedagogy and how it functions. The church inspires the Catholic school in its catholicity, yes; but the Catholic school is not supposed to be a propagandist for the church.

Furthermore, from its inception, the Catholic university "...has always been recognized as an incomparable center of creativity and dissemination"

(1). Again, such attributes that are encouraged by the church can only be realized to the degree it can be an educational institution with the freedom to unfold the faith of the church as it seeks understanding and truth.

There are those in the institutional church, including some bishops, who do not act in accord with these clear guidelines and vision of John Paul II. They treat Catholic educational institutions as if they are supposed to be a propaganda arm for Catholicism. They attempt to control what and how the Catholic schools teach and who and what students can study. This certainly does not respect what the church has said about the mission of Catholic education. Again, there is a disconnect between what has been espoused by the institutional church regarding Catholic schools and some of the present attempts to control how those schools act.

Speaking of the mission of the Catholic university, Pope John Paul II observed, "Their mission appears increasingly necessary for the encounter of the church with the development of the sciences and with the cultures of our age" (10). Most important in understanding how a Catholic school should do this, Pope John Paul II bluntly state, "It possesses that institutional autonomy necessary to perform its functions effectively and guarantees its members academic freedom, so long as the rights of the individual person and of the community are preserved within the confines of the truth and the common good" (12).

Further in the document, the pope states, "Bishops should encourage the creative work of theologians" (29), "…to promote a continuous and profitable dialogue between the Gospel and modern society" (45). Also very important in understanding the role of Catholic education, he clearly posits, "Catholic teaching and discipline are to influence all university activities, while the freedom of conscience of each person is to be fully respected" (part 2, article 2.4).

These characteristics and ideals professed by the Supreme Pontiff of the Catholic Church, Pope John Paul II, magnificently capture what Catholic education should be all about. However, instead of a spirit of creative empowerment and encouragement, the institutional church lately has placed a pall of intrusive and scrutinizing actions over Catholic education and educators. This type of interaction does not bring about the spirit of *Ex Corde Ecclesiae*, nor does it respect the institutional autonomy that John Paul II proclaimed so eloquently.

In this book, I will present some recent experiences of my colleagues while administering in Catholic educational institutions. The specific educators and institutions are not identified by name. There is currently enough tension between Catholic educational institutions and the institutional church without adding to their burdens. Neither is any particular individual within the hierarchy singled out, since there are many bishops who are tremendous supporters, helping to sustain and encourage Catholic educators. We have some reason to hope that Pope Francis will be among them. However, these examples of institutional church attempts to control Catholic schools by insisting that they are an integral part of the church rather than "born from the heart of the church" are pervasive enough to cause significant difficulties for Catholic education and will be familiar to those aware of present-day circumstances in operating Catholic schools.

For instance, how does the Catholic school foster an "impartial search for the truth," if the particular diocese in which it is located will not permit the educators to decide on the reading materials that are used in the school, especially in religion classes? For example, there are strict and narrow guidelines that are being placed on Catholic schools in which the use of "inclusive language" is extremely limited in religion texts.

In some Catholic schools there is strict control on the discussion of other controversial topics that critics do not accept as suitable to be even addressed in a Catholic school. The result of this censorship of materials is that students— who have complete and easy access to all and every forbidden topic *outside* of the Catholic school—are allowed to be addressed *inside* the Catholic school only to be handed the official church teaching on the issue, without nuance or inspection or introspection.

The unwanted result—even for the people who are pushing this approach— is to prevent faithful and professional Catholic educators from accompanying their students in their search for understanding. They cannot share the Catholic viewpoint on controversial questions when there is only one version of the truth. Then there is no real need for education, only indoctrination. The current Chinese government, for example, seems to have adopted this course in their educational system. Must the Catholic Church do the same?

This situation has become a significant problem in Catholic schools and universities around the world. Students can, do, and will uncover and discover controversial topics on their own that are present in their society at any particular time. And especially enticing to them are topics that the institutional church even hints are inappropriate or forbidden for them to discuss. The students proceed with their usual click on their computer and study the topic on their own. So instead of these controversial topics being studied with the assistance of professional Catholic educators, they are left to be investigated by the students without informed input as to Catholic values.

In no way is it what John Paul II called an "impartial search for the truth" if the institutional church does not trust its dedicated and committed teachers to do their jobs. What the critics do not seem to understand is that they are actually curtailing the spread of the Catholic faith. They are preventing the Catholic schools from doing their job, which is to make that faith understandable to the new generations of young people who are immersed in a globalized society with competing values.

How does the Catholic school "encounter the cultures of our age," as the pope put it, in schools that are pressured concerning who can make presentations or be given an award, or which plays may be performed, or what artistic expression is acceptable? Catholic schools face a growing amount of tension and intrusive pressures by what I have come to describe as the church's "self-appointed police force." Catholic school and university administrators and faculty are now forced to deal with destructive critics who, instead of encouraging guided educational encounters for students within the cultures of the age, are trying to impose their own ideological prejudices with a patina of religious orthodoxy. I have found that most of these people are usually out of touch with students' lived realities. Once again, it is the church that suffers when these critics are given power, since students then do not receive the best learning experience that a Catholic school can offer its students. Graduates of schools who cave to these pressures must then encounter the competing cultures in our world without the education they came to us for in the first place.

Are these ideologues so naïve and patronizing as to believe that if students do not encounter the world in the Catholic school they then will be shielded miraculously from it? In this age of wide-open communication, this is naïveté that is tantamount to criminal negligence. And, compounding this destructive tension in today's Catholic schools and universities, there is clear support in some dioceses for this type of self-appointed policing of Catholic adult education. (It is interesting, however, that the institutional church does not appreciate it when those same ideologues police its own actions and determine that even the hierarchy and the Vatican are not "Catholic enough" for them.)

How can the institutional church justify its actions regarding Catholic educational institutions in light of John Paul II's directive that "Bishops should encourage the creative work of theologians"? For example, any fair-minded observer reviewing the public statements coming from the United States Conference of Catholic Bishops' Committee on Doctrine would be hard pressed to understand their strong attacks against certain theologians (especially, if I may say it, women) who exhibit any creativity in their scholarly research and writings. Ask theologians in most Catholic schools and universities if they feel supported and encouraged by the institutional church "to promote a continuous and profitable dialogue between the Gospel and modern society." I think you already know their answer.

> *There is a significant and continual disconnect between so many of the magnificent and inspiring exhortations of the church about Catholic education and how Catholic schools are being treated today.*

What I am saying is that there is a significant and continual disconnect between so many of the magnificent and inspiring exhortations of the church about Catholic education and how Catholic schools are being treated today. And when the people see this, they are dismayed at the difference between what the institutional church preaches about Catholic education and what it currently practices.

Finally, Pope John Paul II explicitly states that a Catholic educational institution must have the "…institutional autonomy to perform its functions effectively" (12). Of course, there is no doubt or argument that the Catholic university, which is "born from the heart of the

Church," is inspired by and embraced by the church. Catholic schools and universities have an awesome responsibility to be faithful to the church, but that faithfulness unfolds in an efficacious and unique way. A Catholic school's institutional autonomy does not negate its faithfulness to the church. Its freely chosen Catholic identity is in communion with and inspired by the church. But a school is not a church. It exists, works, interacts, and is committed to the "... People of God and the human family" (13.4) in a unique way that is proper to a school, not a church.

That is all I am trying to say.

CHAPTER THREE

How Is the Catholic School Catholic?

• • • • • •

It is not religious because of its faith,
but because of the quality of its doubt.

T.S. ELIOT
(commenting on Tennyson's "In Memorium")

• • • • • •

In the Gospel according to Matthew (18:1–5), the disciples were quarrelling among themselves about some of the timely and contentious topics on their minds. Here it is, at the very beginnings of the church, and those very leaders that Jesus had just recently selected to receive the "keys to the kingdom" are already disagreeing with one another: Who is more important? Who should be the boss? Who is the greatest? Indeed, the church did not have to wait for two thousand years to experience differences and disagreements within its ranks. Why should the institutional church be surprised that these same types of questions and differences are present today?

These questions among the chosen twelve were not ones that most would expect coming from Christ's apostles. Questions that would have seemed to be more appropriate might have been: How can we serve your people better, Jesus? How do we show our compassion and love to those in distress, Jesus? How do we embrace the sinner, Jesus? How can we teach as you have taught us, Jesus?

But these were not the questions they asked the Son of God, who was in their very presence. So, from very beginning of his church, Jesus witnessed the human proclivity to the tensions of authority and power found in all institutional dynamics. Jesus lived in first-century Palestine, where he saw his own people in the awful quandary of those times: to serve Rome or to serve God. Is it any wonder, then, that God's infinite wisdom elicited the need to send the Holy Spirit to guide and grace the church and all the People of God?

However, what is essential in Matthew's account is how Jesus took his disciples beyond the story and taught them an important Christian truth. In fact, I contend emphatically that this particular story should mark the beginning of the Catholic school, with Jesus as the first Catholic school teacher!

In this case, without resorting to rigid or defined doctrinal propositions, Jesus places a child in the middle of this chosen group of twelve apostles (the first bishops of the church) and tells them, "Unless you become as this child you will not enter into the kingdom of heaven."

Reflecting on this passage, Archbishop Jean-Louis Bruguès, OP, then Secretary of the Congregation for Catholic Education, in a homily given in the Generalate of the De LaSalle Brothers, Rome, May 14, 2010, beautifully captured the essence of Matthew's story when he said, "The Gospel does not recommend any kind of infantile regression; it does not seek to make us stupid or naïve. No, the child presented by Jesus is a fragile and dependent creature, who needs others to support him in order to become himself."

As teacher, Jesus models for all to see what it means to be Catholic educators in schools that come from "the heart of the church." Catholic schools are to give support to the fragile and the dependent. They are to be neither the monitor nor the doctrinal police of those entrusted to their care. Nor are they meant to view themselves as the dogma and doctrine enforcers for the church. This is a fairly radical view of Catholic education, but I believe it is the correct one, and I am going to try to prove it to you.

The Catholic school and its teachers should accompany the children of God of all ages on their individual journey to meaningfulness and knowledge. It is a journey that should propel students by using the basic principles of Catholic faith to seek understanding of the real world in which they live. As Archbishop Bruguès pointed out, "We are invited, therefore, to recognize ourselves also as children, sons and daughters of the same Father, whose providential teaching supports us so that we can become ourselves, fulfilling the dream that God has planned for each one of us."

Thus, the Catholic school does not impose the church's truth and the Gospel message on its students. It unfolds the faith within a context of the student's pursuit of knowledge, as that student is guided by, and in relationship to, God's grace. In the Catholic school—from primary grades to university level classes—students must be totally free to seek, to question, and to embrace their own doubts and convictions within a spirit of the total freedom of inquiry implied by the phrase *faith seeking understanding.*

• • • • • •

Students must be totally free to seek, to question, and to embrace their own doubts and convictions.

• • • • • •

The institutional church, for its part, must extend its encouragement and support to the Catholic school with the same understanding that it has publicly professed when it mandates that we should teach as Jesus did, who said: "Anyone who welcomes in my name a child like this welcomes me."

This approach to Catholic education offers a quite different role for the Catholic school from that of the Catholic Church. As Archbishop Bruguès further elaborated on this point in his homily, "Christian education is also an education in freedom.… Young people are our teachers because they dislodge us from ourselves; they drag us out of the private spaces where we have piled up our certainties, convictions, and even our tiredness of life. To our eyes, often clouded by the evils of our age, they stress the positive things about our society and its culture." Indeed children have much to teach all of us, especially the leaders of Catholic education and the institutional church. Our students are not empty tablets on which we are to write the truth as we know it. They are participants in their own education—and ours.

What can be gleaned from Jesus' story of the child is that a Catholic school is Catholic if it teaches as Jesus did; if it gives support to the fragile and dependent; if it encourages its students to become people who know they are gifted by God; if it educates its students to freedom; if they see the young as those who also teach us; and if they prevent us from claiming and peddling false certitude about life's basic questions and mysteries.

Given the progress of science and knowledge and the pluralistic global world in which the church must proclaim the Gospel, the Catholic school can help the institutional church unravel itself from its present quandary, but only if Catholic schools are allowed and encouraged to educate students into a faith that recognizes a world of competing values. This cannot happen unless the Catholic school can educate its students in an open and free way that brings to its students an understanding and a context of the competing values, viewpoints, and cultural differences abounding in modern society.

Anytime anyone or any institution, under the guise of paternalistic or maternalistic concern, shields a child from information or knowledge of competing values in the world, it is a hindrance to that child's growth in a strong, adult faith. All that is left for that child is to worry about who is the most important, the boss, the greatest—because they have missed the point. They must become like little children and be allowed to explore the world.

Especially in our third millennium world of total information overload, this approach is key to the New Evangalization Pope Benedict XVI called for. People are not meant to be immature in their faith. The church and the Catholic school should not keep people at a childish level when in every other arena in their lives they are expected to be thinking and mature individuals. That is not what Jesus meant by telling the apostles to become like little children. Little children explore and create and test and learn without fear—if that is allowed by their teachers.

Limiting students to ask only questions that are deemed appropriate and limiting dialogue on any topic of student inquiry is neither real education nor is it effective Christian formation. It is indoctrination; it is distrust in the working of the Spirit; it is an attempt to control. In today's world on this shrinking globe, Catholic teachings and values cannot take hold unless those with life's most important questions—the children—have a safe, secure, and non-judgmental place to ask those questions. The Catholic school can be that place. Catholic teaching cannot happen unless a good Catholic school helps and nurtures those entrusted to its care by situating the Christian faith in an intellectual and pastoral setting that helps its students understand authentic Catholic teaching in the context of a real world of competing ideologies, values, and religions.

Of course, in order for Catholic schools to really be Catholic, they must accept the duty and responsibility to honestly and clearly present Catholic teaching. They must not represent something which is contrary to the church's *magisterium* as Catholic teaching. But Catholic schools must be places where open and candid discussions are encouraged. The notion that "if we don't talk about something controversial, the faithful will not question it" is simply mistaken. Does the institutional church actually believe that most of the faithful have no questions or doubts about its positions on birth control, abortion, gay marriage, divorce and remarriage, or other issues pertaining to sexuality and procreation, and surely, myriad other concerns?

• • • • • •

Catholic schools must be places where open and candid discussions are encouraged.

• • • • • •

The institutional church must accept that the Catholic school has a commitment and dedication to the Catholic faith and that is exactly why it is a good place for the questioning student to ask questions. Just because controversial topics are discussed in a Catholic school does not mean that it supports values and positions contrary to the Catholic faith. The Catholic educator understands quite well that allowing open and candid discussion does not mean advocating a position that is contrary to Catholic values. Free and open discourse that fosters thoughtful intellectual inquiry is essential in any kind of school and especially in Catholic schools. Such honesty and openness cannot be seen as advocacy of anti-Catholic values. Of course the Catholic school must ensure the professional and appropriate training of its teachers to facilitate such open discussions. The training should be about precisely how to have such open conversations, not about how *not* to have them!

Without this kind of openness, a Catholic school lacks appropriate and essential academic freedom. The Catholic school has a professional and moral responsibility to teach an authentic and reliable version of Catholic theology and values as enunciated by the *magisterium* of the church. This does not preclude the Catholic school from accompanying its students in a dialogue of competing viewpoints, ideologies, religions, and secular culture. In the process of having these dialogues, Catholic educators must not be marked with labels such as *conservative* or *liberal*—this is a disservice to the committed and dedicated Catholic educators serving these institutions and ultimately the church. Some Catholic school teachers and administrators will, of necessity, have different personal views on a variety of Catholic teachings. Guess what? They mirror the entire People of God in this regard. But that does not mean they cannot accurately present the church's teaching and moderate a discussion of other views.

Remember: a Catholic school is not the Catholic Church, and the Catholic Church is not a Catholic school. If a pope, for example, says that women can never be ordained or gay people can never be married and that the matter should not be discussed further, that is the institutional church's position on that issue. If a Catholic educator is asked about the same question by a student, he or she should be able to state the church's position clearly and without bias. But that should not prevent the teacher from exploring with the student what others are saying about that issue, both inside and outside the Catholic Church. Were the pope to do that same thing, he would be acting as a teacher, not as the official spokesman for the church.

The institutional church must make real the U.S. bishops' recent call, "in all things charity." Catholic education can truly assist the church in reaching the young people entrusted to it, but only to the degree that it is permitted and encouraged to be a school—not the church—and exist in *communio* with the sense of that profound charity. An important aspect of these very points was emphasized by Pope Benedict XVI on September 17, 2010, when he said in his address to British society at Westminster Hall, "This is why I would suggest that the world of secular rationality and the world of religious belief need one another, and should not be afraid to enter into profound and ongoing dialogue for the good of our civilization." Where can this be done, if not in a school, especially a Catholic school?

CHAPTER FOUR

"Tikkun Olam"—Repair the World!

. . . . . .

The common good concerns the life of all.
It calls for prudence from each, and even more
from those who exercise the office of authority....
The order of things must be subordinate to the order of persons,
and not the other way around.

The Catechism of the Catholic Church

. . . . . .

A legitimate question that arises among Catholic educators is what they can do to help the institutional church move beyond its current quandary. Yet they know that they must do this while remaining faithful to their own mission to educate their students in an evolving, diverse world of competing cultures, values, and religions. It is not an easy task sometimes for the Catholic school to convince all its varied constituencies, within and outside the church, of its validity to call itself "Catholic" and yet at the same time convince the general public of its validity as a qualified and professional educational institution in its own right.

Faith seeking understanding is a concept difficult enough for students if they are only viewing their own Catholic faith. The added bombardment, by instantaneous and mass media, presenting diverse faiths and belief systems exploding right in front of them as they click into the world on their computers or cell phones does not make the task any easier for the Catholic school.

Again one should recall that the church's main focus is to *proclaim* the Gospel (in a religious sense), while the Catholic school should *explain* it (in an existential sense). Think of it this way: *proclaiming* is to *explaining* as *information* is to *formation*. Each focus is important and dependent on the other in the learning process. However, each utilizes qualitatively different approaches in its focus in order to be effective within its respective milieu; even though the objective for the church and the school is ultimately formation of the whole person, they are arrived at in different ways.

To proclaim the Gospel involves the mysterious and spiritual world of God's revelation to humanity: the main focus of the church. However, explaining this divinely inspired revelation involves exploring how faith seeks understanding in a world of empirical data. This distinction is an essential obligation for the Catholic school to understand and embrace.

• • • • • •

It is not the school's objective to proselytize and indoctrinate its students.

• • • • • •

It is true that information concerning the deposit of faith of the Catholic Church is important for the Catholic school to teach. It must inform its students accurately and totally as to that content. However, it is not the school's objective to proselytize and indoctrinate its students in the sense of being responsible or insuring that the students become lifetime adherents to the faith. That is the job of the church.

In essence the distinction may be justified with this understanding. Both the Catholic Church and the Catholic school are intimately involved with evangelization (i.e. to share the good news of the Gospel of Jesus Christ); but the focus of the church in this regard is the formation of its faithful in order to bring Christ to the people through the church, while the focus for the Catholic school is to educate its students in order to bring Christ to all people through the various cultures the students will touch throughout their lives. Of course both are concerned with humanity embracing the invitation of Christ to be his followers. How that is accomplished, however, involves significantly different approaches and a qualitatively different context.

Here is a way of thinking about this. If a Protestant or Jewish or Muslim or Hindu or Buddhist or atheist or agnostic student wants to attend a Catholic school (at any level), should that be allowed? Most would answer that question affirmatively. Certainly most Catholic colleges cannot operate without non-Catholic students, but most elementary and secondary Catholic institutions also welcome non-Catholic students, not only to build up their student body but also to provide it a much-desired diversity.

Now the question is whether the school should try to convert those non-Catholic students. Most would say no. That is the job of the church, not the school. On the other hand, should non-Catholic students be excused from religion or theology classes, or should Catholic views be eliminated from the study of subjects such as literature or history or the social sciences? Most would object to that as well. If it is a Catholic school, there should be an expectation that the Catholic faith should be clearly and positively presented to all the students, but without the expectation that the students—Catholic and non-Catholic alike—would automatically become good, practicing Catholics at the end of their course of study. That is simply not the job of any school in any faith.

In seeking this balanced approach, it is good to keep in mind the keen observation made by the accomplished and insightful theologian Gabriel Moran: "It is not the truth that divides us but the claim to the truth." And, as an extension of this thought, Pope Benedict XVI made a similar observation when he was speaking to representatives of other religions at St. Mary's University College, Twickenham, England, on September 17, 2010: "The dialogue of life involves simply being alongside one another and learning from one another in such a way as to grow in mutual knowledge and respect."

Following in this chapter is my attempt to present an educational process and vision that Catholic educators should consider that will help all their students—Catholic and non-Catholic alike—respect and interact with a world filled with diverse people and beliefs—a future that is actually present right now in a globalized society in a shrinking modern world.

This chapter relies on and utilizes the excellent research of Cynthia A. Nienhaus, CSA, PhD, in her theological study presented for her doctoral dissertation titled, "Transformation of the World: Covenant-Centric Christian

Religious Education." Although this work utilizes her extensive and thorough research in this subject area, it is important to state clearly that its application in this work was not necessarily Sister Nienhaus' intention. I accept full responsibility for the manner that her fine scholarship is used herein.

The context of these insights is significantly dependent on the work of Isaac Luria, a sixteenth-century rabbi and Jewish mystic, who is considered to be the father of contemporary *Kabbalah*. Kabbalah is an aspect found within Rabbinic Judaism concerned with explaining the relationship between the Creator of the universe and the universe itself.

To situate a covenant-centric focus for Catholic education, Professor Nienhaus relates a metaphorical Kabbalistic story in Jewish mysticism involving an understanding about the creation of the world: "The Breaking of the Vessels" (*shevirat hakelim* in Hebrew). In this account, God formed ten vessels, each containing light. However, as God was pouring this light into the vessels, seven of them broke and shattered. Consequently each of the seven vessels containing bits of this Divine Light were scattered throughout the universe. God then directed humanity to find these broken pieces and to restore them as they were before creation.

Several important aspects about creation are related in this story. First, the sanctity of creation is emphasized, and this sanctity is even found in those broken and fragmented parts of creation. Second, we can see in this account that the world from its very beginnings experienced brokenness and destruction. Third, the story unfolds the insight that God desires a covenantal relationship with humanity, since God relies on people to repair these broken vessels and return them to the original state filled with light.

As God relies on people to repair these vessels, what, in fact, God wants is for people to help "repair the fabric of the world"—or in Hebrew *tikkun olam*. In essence, Nienhaus is strongly recommending that Catholic education in its totality—not solely in its religious education—should transform its self-understanding of its mission to embrace the repair of the fabric of the world as its strikingly signal attribute in service to the church and for the world. The Catholic school can proclaim peace and prosperity to the degree that it sees itself as serving humanity through educating each and every one of its students to repair the fabric of the world. The Jewish theologian, David Ellenson, said it well in his book, *Building a World in Which God Would Be Happy to Live*:

> God is in need of each of us if holiness is to be achieved in the world. Our actions have cosmic import. The very presence of God in the world is dependent upon what you and I do.

If Catholic educators develop and explore this covenantal type of self-understanding of their mission as they conduct their schools—whether on the primary, secondary, special education, or university levels—they will become a beacon of light not only for future secular education but also for the fruition of what is best for a Catholic school in the third millennium. Sister Nienhaus says it so well in her research when she describes covenant-centric education in these terms:

> Through the initial act and the ongoing acts of creation, God shows a desire to maintain a personal and covenantal relationship with all people throughout all time…. Participating in a covenantal relationship can enable people to be co-creators with God in the ongoing acts of the creation of the world.

The importance of this understanding cannot be overemphasized on this globe, whose shrinking has been precipitated by the technological revolution. This covenant-centric understanding of education emphasizes the relationship that God establishes with all human beings, and it is not sectarian, nor is it only in the domain of the institutional church. The emphasis falls on the personal call and response between the person and the Creator in order to repair the fabric of the world. The Catholic school, then, should situate its mission with the understanding that this covenant relationship excludes no one: Catholic education is for all people.

Indeed, it is not an exaggeration that this *tikkun olam* focus for Catholic education even has credibility for other religions, and even for the secularists. Respect for creation engenders values that support respect for the dignity of humanity, the protection of the environment, dialogue among people, and acceptance of diversity in the world.

In order for understanding and peace to have a chance to become a reality in the globalized world of competing values, education must play a more significant role than ever before throughout the entire world. And with this focus, Catholic education can become the exemplar and new paradigm for all educational institutions. If people are to be prepared to repair the fabric of the world, then they must be educated to dynamic learning possibilities that encourage empathy and solidarity among human beings.

There is also, of course, an even easier facilitation possible when the focus is primarily concerned with the Catholic faith. A covenant-centric educational focus for Catholic schools can easily emphasize the Catholic teachings and traditions around the principle of *Imago Dei*, i.e., that all people are created in God's image. Thomas Groome stated this aspect clearly and eloquently in his book, *Educating for Life: A Spiritual Vision for Every Teacher and Parent*:

• • • • • •

People must be educated to dynamic learning possibilities that encourage empathy and solidarity among humanity.

• • • • • •

The *Imago Dei* tenet witnesses not only to the essential goodness of persons, but also to the equal dignity of all human beings—men and women; people of every color, class and creed. As reflections of God, all have an essential dignity that gives them the "birthright" to be treated with reverence and with dignity befitting a daughter or son of God. All human beings have innate rights to what is needed to become fully alive persons, and they have corresponding responsibilities to maintain the rights of others—to live for life for all.

In the diversified world of today, Catholic schools can foster an open and free environment that would accommodate a plurality of interactions, if they choose this approach. The constant value would always be to respect religious pluralism while clearly articulating the Catholic deposit of faith.

However, the hierarchy and institutional church do not always accept this approach with Catholic schools or theologians. Many times there is public criticism against the Catholic school or theologian attempting to foster an openness and respect and appreciation of a pluralism of views. Theologian Peter Phan received criticism when he wrote the following in his essay, "Religious Identity and Belonging Amidst Diversity and Pluralism:"

> Religious pluralism then is not just a matter of fact but also a matter of principle. That is, non-Christian religions may be seen as part of the plan of divine Providence and endowed with a particular role in the history of salvation. They are not merely a "preparation'" for, "stepping stone" toward, or "seeds" of Christianity and destined to be fulfilled by it. Rather they have their own autonomy and their proper role as ways of salvation, at least for their adherents.

Given the pluralistic society that is the one and only reality in which all the inhabitants on this globe now live, the Catholic school should accept the challenge to effectively educate its students within a covenant-centric focus with the noble intention to repair the the fabric of the world. Yes, it will at times be misunderstood and criticized. But Catholic educators should muster the courage to do take on that challenge.

Catholic schools do *not* educate their students into the rich Catholic intellectual tradition that is their heritage if they ignore the pluralistic reality of the world as it is. Catholic schools *will be deficient* if they do not fully educate their students so that they are intellectually and maturely equipped to live in this world and help repair its very fabric.

The Catholic school can do all this and still teach authentic Catholic doctrine, morals, and principles. Furthermore, the Catholic faith cannot be taught effectively unless theologians are encouraged to situate the Catholic deposit of faith within an intellectual infrastructure for the third millennium global society.

All this can be accomplished if the hierarchy and the institutional church—

as a whole—support, trust, and encourage Catholic schools in this *tikkun olam* perspective of covenant-centric education. This will also help the institutional church significantly evaluate their current standing in the education community and lead the way to their own *metanoia* that will aid them in unraveling the quandary that they themselves are experiencing. (*Metanoia* is the Greek word meaning repentance and conversion through a change of heart and mind toward virtue.)

If this kind of cooperation is not forthcoming from the institutional church, then Catholic educators should not wait until that happens. Rather, they should make these changes in their schools if they are not fully focused in this way. They should do this while faithfully, patiently, and respectfully hoping that, eventually, the institutional church will see the light that returns to those broken vessels spoken of in the *Kabbalah* tradition. It would be those very vessels that the Catholic schools would be repairing in cooperation with the Creator's covenant.

CHAPTER FIVE

Dueling Intellectual Traditions in Catholicism

• • • • • •

Trust the Church to answer more questions than any other institution about life's baffling problems. But do not expect her to answer them all, for there are questions to which there is no answer this side of eternity.

MSGR. JOHN TRACY ELLIS

• • • • • •

Whether from church prelates at the Vatican, bishops around the world, teachers in elementary and secondary schools, administrators and professors in universities, or Catholic intellectuals in general, one can often hear comments regarding "the Catholic intellectual tradition." Many individuals and groups speak as if there were one, and only one, Catholic intellectual tradition, and even more amazing they claim that they, and only they, possess it. The Catholic intellectual tradition is, indeed, a rich and unique phenomenon that has enriched untold numbers of people seeking a holistic meaning of humanity and the world. But the property of any one individual or group it is not!

The intellectual tradition of faith seeking understanding, as the process unfolds within the world's evolving globalized society, is truly remarkable. Yet there seems to be a widening gap developing between the Catholic intellectual tradition as embraced by the institutional church and that which is practiced in Catholic education.

To use the word *tradition* in an appropriate manner in this context is a very important requirement. Tradition, according to Catholic theology, is one of the two sources of divine Revelation, along with Sacred Scripture. Tradition comes from the lived experience of the faithful, the *sensus fidelium*. When the People of God attempt to unfold their foundational principles in order to nurture their intellectual life, they should be fully aware that the knowledge and wisdom that they seek are inspired by the Catholic faith in a two-millenium-plus context of reason, exploration, and worldly intelligibility.

Though there is usually a reluctance to highlight actual differences in the intellectual life between the institutional church and Catholic educational institutions, it is nevertheless very important to do so. Some may even argue that Catholic intellectual tradition is the same for both, but I believe the opposite. Reluctance to discuss these differences, or sometimes even to admit that these differences exist, arises because the Catholic educator does not want to appear disloyal to the institutional church by pointing out these differences and cause even more tension than already exists.

• • • • • •

The institutional church must remember its past so that it can bring validity to its historical roots in the person of Jesus Christ.

• • • • • •

The institutional church, first and foremost, must remember its past so that it can bring validity to its historical roots in the person of Jesus Christ, the incarnate Word and Savior of the world. Jesus not only lived some two thousand years ago as a historical person, he is as real now as a presence in the world as he was then. The church, as it embraces this mystery, is necessarily steeped in its intellectual traditions, through its liturgies, sacraments, music, art, teachings, and all of its other facets. The job of the institutional church is to preserve and proclaim the sacred mysteries entrusted to its care in the best ways it can.

Not one Catholic educator I know believes that life and the world can be solely mastered through empirically verifiable facts that are found in science. As observed previously, however, unlike the institutional church, the Catholic school must engage their students within the culture. The institutional church should be just as concerned as the school is to ensure that faith is understood and intelligible within a specific culture and to all people within a particular society. Yet, the institutional church must focus on the deposit of faith and the universal dogmas and doctrines that emanate from that content. The Catholic school, on the other hand, must make that revelation understandable to its students and allow them to question it.

As elaborated more fully below, the Catholic school explores the content of faith in a way that involves determining what is called "proximate truth." It comes from a model that is more democratic, academic, and humanly relational. This process precipitates a real and distinctive difference in Catholic intellectual tradition from that manifest in the institutional church. This is not to say one is better than the other; rather one is clearly *different from* the other in the intellectual processes utilized and the ends each respectively serves. However, what the institutional church needs to accept—but is increasingly fighting—is that these two distinctive intellectual traditions are not opposed to each other but rather are complementary.

When explaining Catholic intellectual tradition, the word *tradition* can be quite elusive and misunderstood. Tradition may conjure in the listener's mind something that is old, past, and static. A correct reading and understanding of Catholic intellectual tradition within the Catholic educational realm should have no resemblance to that understanding of tradition whatsoever. Here are several elements of Catholic intellectual tradition and how they are being handled now by the institutional church.

1. Catholic educational intellectual tradition encourages and fosters a search for truth in dialogue with the world and the culture.

Tradition, as used to describe the Catholic intellectualism that is dominant in Catholic educational institutions, is a different variety and persuasion than that which is common in the institutional church. To understand this difference, one should recall the institutional church's strong intellectual forces that reacted against what they considered destructive, immoral, and hostile modern ideas developing in the 19th-century societies and cultures. The term often used to describe this intellectual movement, which was especially directed toward Catholic theology, is *neo-scholastic reasoning*. This approach involves a significant emphasis on the use of abstract concepts distilled from the works of

Thomas Aquinas.

In today's institutional church, Aquinas, a 13th-century philosopher and theologian who was a Dominican priest, is still one of the most influential thinkers affecting its intellectual tradition. He has the official title of "Doctor of the Church." Because the institutional church over the years has developed its intellectual processes within a neo-scholastic framework that did not take into account the medieval context of Thomas' thinking, the church tends, even today, to pronounce truth in absolute terms. This intellectual approach manifested itself in propositions that try to describe truth in ahistorical and immutable terms. Within the institutional church today, it is widely seen that the vestiges of this more institutionally rigid intellectual tradition are still prevalent and protectively guarded as the favored language, to be accepted by all when speaking of the faith. The institutional church is not at all accommodating to an intellectual exploration that embraces a more diverse and pluralistic manner of approaching Christianity in general, and certainly it is even more resistive to this when approaching Catholicism in particular.

This intellectual approach is quite problematic and the cause of much tension between the institutional church and the Catholic school, however, given a different intellectual tradition that is found in most Catholic educational institutions. The hallmark of Catholic educational intellectual tradition emphasizes an acceptance of nuance and differences within a more diverse variety of content, emanating from direct contact with students and research in contemporary cultures. This transformation was engendered in the new wave of reform ushered in by Vatican II in the early 1960s. Instead of focusing on truth in absolute terms and seeking immutable intellectual constructs, Catholic education, encouraged by Vatican II's *aggiornamento* (opening windows, so to speak), emphasized the study and research of human experience and its relational dynamics to God's grace in the world.

Just how these tensions caused by conflicting intellectual traditions developed in the church since Vatican II can be seen in some public confrontations, almost all initiated by the institutional church. For example, theologian Edward Schillebeeckx, a Belgian priest, like Thomas Aquinas, was a member of the Dominican Order. He was a very influential advisor to bishops participating in Vatican II. After the Council, he continued to explore Vatican II themes through his research, lectures, and writings.

However, in Schillebeeckx's reflections on those themes, he started to introduce practical implications that followed logically from his ideas and required significant changes in how the institutional church was operating. He opened dialogue and questioning regarding how the church should function in more democratic ways as a result of Vatican II teachings. He also sought a more personal approach and greater emphasis on human experience that would be more responsive to Vatican II. Specifically, he dared to suggest that the priestly ordination for those who are married and for women should be open to discussion in the institutional church.

As a result, great pressure was placed upon Schillebeeckx to stop such research. In fact, from the late 1960s until the beginning of the 1980s, three separate official Vatican investigations were conducted about his writings, suggesting that his ideas might be heretical. Although no formal decrees were issued suggesting that his research and studies were heresy, nevertheless, for a period of over a decade, an oppressive intellectual culture caused fear within Catholic educational circles.

2. Catholic educational intellectual tradition seeks to achieve an integration of knowledge through utilization of all academic disciplines and scientific study.

Except for the very rare instances in which there is the formal claim of speaking infallibly, *ex cathedra*, the institutional church should accept the reasonableness of evolving human understanding unfolding in history. However, recent institutional church leaders have had difficulty in accepting this point of view. In their sacred responsibility to teach the truth of God's church, they have been unnecessarily protective and rigid. As a result, even while recognizing the institutional church's best intentions, Catholic educational institutions have been inappropriately restricted from carrying out their search for integration of knowledge in an unencumbered, open, and responsible manner.

For example, consider that in 2010 the U.S. Conference of Catholic Bishops' (USCCB) Committee on Doctrine forcefully criticized the respected and credible research of Creighton University theologians Michael Lawler and Todd Salzman. Their research, published by Georgetown University Press in a book entitled, *The Sexual Person: Toward a Renewed Catholic Anthropology*, received many positive reviews by prominent Catholic theologians and scholars. The book challenges two principles of the official Catholic position on sexuality: that any human genital act must occur within the framework of heterosexual marriage and that each and every marriage act must remain open to the transmission of life. Instead, the authors emphasize relationships, not acts. Professor Julie Hanlon Rubio of St. Louis University praised the book as being "...among the most important works in Catholic sexual ethics to emerge in the last two decades." In addition, the Catholic Press Association cited this work, giving it first honors in its theological category of awards. Indeed, this and all such responsible research and scholarship demonstrate the intellectual tradition of Catholic education, namely, that it seeks to achieve an integration of knowledge through utilization of all academic disciplines and scientific study.

Then consider that in 2011 the same USCCB Committee on Doctrine sharply criticized Sister Elizabeth Johnson's acclaimed book *Quest for the Living God* as "incompatible with Catholic teaching." Sister Johnson stated: "I want to make it absolutely clear that nothing in this book dissents from the church's faith about God revealed in Jesus Christ through the Spirit." It is this very book that the Catholic Theological Society of America recently supported as exhibiting excellent scholarship. In fact, after reviewing the criticism of the Committee on Doctrine, many scholars questioned whether its members actually read Johnson's book.

Also, consider that in a written document dated March 30, 2012, the Vatican's Congregation for the Doctrine of the Faith and approved by Pope Benedict XVI forcefully criticized Sister Margaret Farley's scholarly book *Just Love: A Framework for Christian Sexual Ethics*. Farley is a highly regarded and respected theologian. Many Catholic scholars and theologians consider her book one of the best works available on sexual ethics. She said that the Congregation's criticism "...misrepresents—perhaps unwittingly—the aims of my work and the nature of it as a proposal that might be in service, not against, the church and its faithful people." Yet, Rome says that her book "does not conform to church teaching." Furthermore, the document decrees that Farley's book "cannot be used as a valid expression of Catholic teaching, either in counseling and formation, or in ecumenical and interreligious dialogue."

These are but a few examples that highlight the obvious tensions that exist in the Catholic intellectual traditions between the institutional church and Catholic education. One should be able to observe an uncompromising conviction in both venues that as faith seeks understanding the only objective is truth. Catholic intellectual tradition within Catholic education should question, seek, and explore truth while respecting the faith as the church teaches through the *magisterium*. The institutional church, on the other hand, should trust Catholic educators as they explore that faith and seek truth in an evolving and growing universe of knowledge.

3. The pursuit of knowledge is never complete or static.

A third aspect found in Catholic education intellectual tradition is also somewhat of a "lightning rod" for disagreement with the institutional church. Catholic education's intellectual premise emphasizes that the pursuit of knowledge is never complete or static. In this light, even long-held traditional beliefs are open for scrutiny and exploration as new knowledge evolves and questions arise from people and scholars.

In this paradigm, exploration and discussion is always freely pursued and encouraged. Truth must always be tested in a context of reason and evolving knowledge. That should be the singular aim not only in Catholic educational intellectual pursuits but even more so for the institutional church.

However, the institutional church does not always signal its acquiescence to open and free dialogue. There are numerous examples that clearly demonstrate the institutional church's insistence on its authority vis a vis Catholic schools. However, the Catholic school is not supposed to be the propaganda arm of the institutional church; rather it is an institution "born from the heart of the church" that pursues an intellectual framework shedding light on active faith that is seeking understanding in this world.

An encouraging possibility toward a better working relationship evolving between the institutional church and Catholic education is seen in an address delivered by Bishop Gerald Kicanas at the January 30, 2011 annual meeting of the Association for Catholic Colleges and Universities (*National Catholic Reporter*, Jan. 31, 2011). He pointed out to the attending Catholic university leaders the example of the recently beatified Cardinal John Henry Newman who, "Like you, Newman sought to answer and not to suppress what was erroneous. He was willing to engage attitudes and ideas different from what the church taught because he was confident that the truth would prevail and would benefit from the engagement." Bishop Kicanas then reminded the assembly that Newman, "would emphasize his understanding that the faithful as a whole possess the Spirit and should be listened to. This has much to say on how we exercise our authority."

It is refreshing to hear a Catholic bishop set a tone for a healthy understanding of the distinctive yet mutually complimentary way that Catholic educators and the hierarchy should relate to each other. Bishop Kicanas could not have said it better when he emphasized, "Clearly there needs to be room in an academic community for disagreement, debate, and a clash of ideas even in theology. Such debate and engagement can clarify and advance our understanding. In discussion with local bishops, faculties need to be able to disagree and question with mutual respect." If Bishop Kicanas were truly speaking for all the bishops and they would relate to Catholic educators as he indicates, then indeed Catholic schools could be schools and the church could be church!

4. Catholic intellectual tradition involves an insistence and persistence that the pursuit of all knowledge is for the sake of and benefit of people

There is a fourth aspect of the Catholic educational intellectual tradition that has been consistently present and clearly articulated. It is that the Catholic intellectual tradition involves an insistence and persistence that the pursuit of all knowledge is for the sake of and benefit of people. Deeply embedded in this principle is the belief that each person is created in the image and likeness of

God. Therefore each person is endowed with an inestimable worth and dignity.

Both the institutional church and Catholic education have shared this element of their separate intellectual traditions over the centuries. As such, there is an important difference with the purely secular pursuit of knowledge that stresses the principle "knowledge for the sake of knowledge." Certainly this does not imply that within the intellectual tradition of a secular pursuit of knowledge there is also not a concern for the common good of humankind and creation. Rather, in the Catholic intellectual tradition there exists an emphasis focused on social justice and elaborated to an extensive degree in a well-developed Catholic social ethic.

• • • • • •

In the Catholic intellectual tradition there exists an emphasis focused on social justice and elaborated to an extensive degree in a well-developed Catholic social ethic.

• • • • • •

This Catholic social justice tradition, which has clearly demonstrated its importance by its persistence, has been especially highlighted since 1891, when Pope Leo XIII promulgated his great encyclical *Rerum Novarum* (Concerning New Things). Reflecting Pope Leo's times, the encyclical shows an understanding of the context for the rights and responsibilities of capital and labor. Since then, the church and Catholic scholars, schools and universities together have shaped the intellectual development of a body of social teaching that reflects the use of knowledge for the sake of and benefit of all people.

In 1931, Pope Pius XI presented to the world *Quadragesimo Anno* (Forty Years Later), which showed the effects of greed and concentrated economic power on working people and society. Then, in 1967, Pope Paul VI, in his encyclical *Progressio Populorum* (On the Progress of People) affirmed the rights of poor nations to full human development. In 2009, Pope Benedict XVI sent out to the world *Caritas in Veritate* (Love in Truth), a magnificent synthesis of modern economic realities that shall be discussed in the next chapter.

In between the aforementioned cited documents there were many more contributions made by the church and taught by Catholic educators that added immeasurably to the intellectual tradition of Catholic insistence regarding:

- Primacy of the person.
- The social nature of the person.
- The common good as inseparable from the good of persons.
- Solidarity among humankind.
- Subsidiarity within social organizations.
- Participation of people in organizations as a right.
- The dignity of work.
- Equitable use of goods and wealth.
- Concern for the poor and marginalized.

Thus, in regard to an intellectual tradition involving the use of knowledge with a prominent emphasis on its benefit to humankind, there should be complete harmony on this foundational principle between the institutional church and the Catholic school.

It is important for me to note that there is a great body of magnificent and more in-depth elaboration of the Catholic intellectual tradition than I have room to explore here. The four aspects highlighted here are a synthesis of the most pervasive principles that can bring people to a general understanding of Catholic teaching and perhaps provide an important bridge between the institutional church leaders and Catholic educators.

CHAPTER SIX

Faith and Finance: The Pope Tells It Like It Is

• • • • • •

In and of itself wealth is neutral.
What matters is how it is acquired and for what it is used.

CLEMENT OF ALEXANDRIA

• • • • • •

Pope Benedict's decision to resign the papacy got the headlines, but the potential contribution he made to Catholic education is much more profound and provocative.

Caritas in Veritate (Love in Truth) is an encyclical that was officially published July 7, 2009. In this encyclical, Pope Benedict XVI presents a pragmatic look at global economics in the modern world and tells it like it is. His presentation draws from the Catholic intellectual tradition in which the pursuit of knowledge is for the sake of and benefit of people. With a realistic view of the principles articulated in this encyclical, Catholic schools and universities can greatly assist the institutional church as it exhorts all in the globalized world economy to act justly and ethically in a socially responsible manner.

Let's face it, however. Recent resistance to valid criticism from the faithful, as well as its unacceptable response to the priest sexual-abuse scandals, have caused a significant loss of credibility in the institutional church's ability to be the prime animator of people seeking to transform society. Catholic education can have a vital role to play in this regard. Effective learning strategies that can aid peoples of the world to harness the power of the global economy for the common good is probably the most urgent need on this globe today. Such a pursuit, if successful, could be a primary force in helping the institutional church confront its diminishing loss of standing in the world.

To be effective in this task, Catholic educators, schools, and universities should embrace Pope Benedict's principles as unfolded in *Caritas in Veritate* and help make them relevant and alive to their students and to the world. Through their powerful roles as researcher, teacher, learner, and intellectual community of faith-seeking-understanding, Catholic schools can spread the fire that Pope Benedict has lit with his *Caritas in Veritate*.

It might be helpful to first address what *Caritas in Veritate* is not:

- not an economic set of strategies to be followed, though it certainly has some focus on general directions that should be considered;
- not a set of specific solutions to the economic global crisis or a solution to the social problems that the world is encountering; it does, however, reflect on some interesting visions in that regard;
- not a blueprint or map that will point the way to solve real-world concrete problems, though it is not just a pious exhortation of abstract principles;
- not the church's formulation on how to respond to a definitive action plan for a preferential option for the poor;
- not simply a commemoration of Pope Paul VI's 1967 encyclical *Populorum Progressio* or Pope John Paul II's 1991 *Centesimus Annus*, though both are often quoted and referred to in *Caritas in Veritate*.

Caritas in Veritate is truly a unique and extraordinary document. It can be an indispensable force, a creative dynamic, and a potent catalyst that could help bring the worlds of faith and finance together. It can help make freedom, peace, and prosperity a reality for the new globalized society. It can help make the church's dedication to a preferential option for the poor much more than the subject of a nice homily. It can do all this if Catholic education uses its learning and teaching dynamics to bring these ideas of the former pope to fruition.

On the day after the encyclical was made public, at a general audience held in Paul VI Hall, Pope Benedict spoke about it. During that very time, the heads of state of the G8 were meeting in L'Aquila, a short distance from Rome. In fact, at that Papal audience the Pope asked the people to pray for those at the G8 meeting. Was it fate or coincidence that these distinct worlds of church and government were so close, at least physically, that day? Who knows? Nevertheless, what a potent image emerges when these two distinctive groups are set within a vista of proximity in which the world of finance (the G8 participants) and the world of faith (the Pope's general audience on *Caritas in Veritate*) could almost reach out to each other by merely looking out at each other from their respective horizons—L'Aquila and Rome.

Caritas in Veritate is unique among church documents in its exposition of the church's long history in the development of its social doctrine. Uncharacteristically for Church documents like this, Benedict XVI approached timely situations and problems from a point of view that not only involves theological exhortations but also ventures into dialogue with the world. And he thrust himself right into the middle of many of the most difficult global economic problems.

Benedict XVI broke new ground, not only by choosing certain topics but also by his treatment and worldly insights into those topics. He spoke of technology, micro financing, labor unions, intellectual property rights, the environment, free-markets, agrarian reform, business ethics, world energy problems, migration, and the bureaucratic and costly administration of international organizations. He concluded with a plea for the development of a world governance authority with effective powers.

This is extraordinary. Here one sees a pope who strays from the usual and expected area of spirituality and presents a direct and poignant synthesis about timely economic, political, and worldly topics. Since 1891, with the introduction of *Rerum Novarum*, the popes have always reflected on real-life situations, but rarely with such concreteness, directness, and force as that was employed by Benedict in this document.

The response to *Caritas in Veritate* implies that, because of its unique and extraordinary approach reflecting the world as it is today, there is a real possibility that the disparate worlds of faith and finance might actually be able to come together. This could be the foundation leading to new, creative, innovative, and effective strategies to make real to the world the church's preferential option for the poor, and Catholic schools could be at the cutting edge of this effort.

As Benedict XVI warned in this encyclical, "The risk of our time is that the de facto interdependence of people and nations is not matched by ethical interaction of consciences and minds that would give rise to truly human development" (8). It is in the context of "charity in truth" that "only in truth does charity shine forth, only in truth can charity be authentically lived" (3). The Pope pointed out that "The different aspects of the crisis, its solutions, and any new development that the future may bring, are increasingly interconnected, they imply one another, they require new efforts of holistic understanding and a new humanistic synthesis" (21). With this understanding, "The crisis thus becomes an opportunity for discernment, in which to shape a new vision for the future" (21). This is what Catholic educators do every single day.

This "new humanistic synthesis" and this "new vision of the future"—faith and finance—become the light that can show humankind the path to find a way for "love in truth" in a world that is in desperate need of both. However, this can be a productive partnership to the degree that Catholic educators are not interfered with by ideologues with agendas.

Whether we observe the dynamics in societies, nations, politics, or even religions, we can see the negative and destructive forces precipitated by ideologies of all kinds. Often competing ideologies cause a reductionism in thinking that casts people and institutions into liberal or conservative camps—the left or the right. Then, from those ideological polarities, supposed strategies, values, and principles are twisted and molded to conform to an ideology rather than address the problem at hand. Sides are taken, unnecessary animosity is developed, and the crisis, problem, or situation requiring repair goes unsolved. All too often we see energy to do good and desire for cooperation and creativity dissipate and turn people against people, institution against institution, institutional church against Catholic schools, and one religion against another.

Benedict XVI, in *Caritas in Veritate*, went a long way to correct that situation as he presented his propositions to the world regarding an economic global awareness that will effectively initiate a "new humanistic synthesis" in order "to shape a new vision for the future." He eloquently, decisively, and courageously explored the issue of wealth distribution vs. wealth creation—a topic charged with ideological dynamite in the world of global economics. Without a doubt, the observer will see opponents to Benedict's analysis—whether in politics, business, or in the church itself—try to twist what the Pope said on this subject in order to fit their respective ideologies. No doubt, people will hear many across the globe, shouting from the hilltops, "The Pope is on my side!"

I reject that type of forced reading of *Caritas in Veritate*. The subject of wealth distribution vs. wealth creation is a very important and pragmatic economic concern that must be addressed with an unbiased, non-ideological, fair, and open reading of Benedict XVI's views. I think that any reasonable person who reads this encyclical will see the wisdom of his positions. There must be a reconciliation within the ideological battleground if we are ever to agree upon a "new vision for the future." The pope presented one and there is no better place to work out the details than in Catholic schools.

• • • • • •

There must be a reconciliation within the ideological battleground if we are ever to agree upon a "new vision for the future."

• • • • • •

For instance, Pope Benedict XVI brought up the controversial topic of profit. Rather than take an ideological swipe on one side or the other, he stated simply, "Profit is useful..." (21). However, with keen insight he further clarified that profit is useful in the scheme of human development within society only "...if it serves as a means towards an end that provides a sense both of how to produce it and how to make good use of it" (21). In essence, the Pope produced no anathemas against capitalism, but he held it accountable for what it actually produces.

There are many poignant observations that Benedict XVI made on this important and controversial topic. Probably, the most far-reaching and decisive example in his balanced approach is seen when he talked about free markets —the center and most vital "heart" of the ideological battle that is taking place. Benedict XVI told us with great wisdom and insight:

In a climate of mutual trust, the *market* is the economic institution that permits encounter between persons, inasmuch as they are economic subjects who make use of contracts to regulate their relations as they exchange goods and services of equivalent value between them, in order to satisfy their needs and desires. The market is subject to the principles of so-called *commutative justice*, which regulates the relations of giving and receiving between parties to a transaction. But the social doctrine of the Church has unceasingly highlighted the importance of *distributive justice* and *social justice* for the market economy, not only because it belongs within a broader social and political context but also because of the wider network of relations within which it operates. In fact, if the market is governed solely by the principle of the equivalence in value of exchanged goods, it cannot produce the social cohesion that it requires in order to function well. *Without internal forms of solidarity and mutual trust, the market cannot completely fulfill its proper economic function"* (35).

This passage clearly demonstrates that Benedict XVI objectively assessed the current global economic situation. He did not diminish the church's rich and magnificent social doctrine and its traditional underpinnings dating back to 1891 with Pope Leo XIII's *Rerum Novarum*. Yet he was able to address controversial wealth distribution vs. wealth creation arguments with fairness and balance. If Catholic educators can imitate Benedict in this regard and effectively bring his message to the global economic scene, then they may be able to make a significant contribution toward solving today's global economic mess. Certainly though, if Catholic school leaders buy into the left-right and liberal-conservative fights, the world may well stay in the broken, ineffective, and deteriorating condition in which it finds itself now. The world, more than ever, needs the new vision of faith and finance coming together in an intelligible way for the benefit of global society. And the institutional church, more than ever, needs Catholic educators to take the lead in facilitating this.

Another area that Catholic schools can take the lead in is ethics. Without any trepidation, Benedict XVI announced plainly and clearly, "Corruption and illegality are unfortunately evident in the conduct of the economic and political class in rich countries, both old and new, as well as in poor ones" (22). How wonderful that in one sentence he told all to stop the nonsense of trying to blame the rich or the poor, the developed or undeveloped countries, capitalism or socialism. It is people—corrupt people and people acting illegally, that is the main problem. Without any trepidation, Benedict XVI announced plainly and clearly:

> In and of itself, the market is not, and must not become, the place where the strong subdue the weak. Society does not have to protect itself from the market, as if the development of the latter were, *ipso facto*, to entail the death of authentically human relations. Admittedly, the market can be a negative force, not because it is so by nature, but because a certain ideology can make it so (36).

It is people—dishonest people, who twist reality with false ideologies to the detriment of the weak, the marginalized, and the poor. Again, the Pope told it like it is. Without any trepidation, he insisted, "The economic sphere is neither ethically neutral, nor inherently inhuman and opposed to society. It is part and parcel of human activity and precisely because it is human, it must be structured and governed in an ethical manner" (36). Pope Benedict made it clear that the world of economics and finance is not some necessary evil in this world that people are reluctantly forced to deal with. On the contrary, he clearly states that all economic activity is a significant and constitutive part of being human.

A careful reading of the encyclical presents other examples of Benedict XVI's pragmatic counsel about the complex world of economic activity. Of course, there are those who will give more emphasis to his theological, philosophical, and spiritual elaborations. All these dimensions are, indeed, found there; but in order to focus on Catholic schools it is important to stress that in *Caritas in Veritate* Benedict XVI's head was not in the clouds of unrealistic goals. The Pope was talking, sharing, and counseling the world about real-life, human development concerns in today's globalized society: an absolute necessity for both faith and finance.

My greatest fear, especially for those in the Catholic education community, is that instead of putting into action what Benedict was clearly saying, we will continue to argue about what it is he said. We will all be led astray by carving *Caritas in Veritate* into a monument to fit a particular ideology. Catholic schools must prevent that from happening.

Pope Benedict XVI has now retired. The job he identified of fixing this "earthly city" is properly in the domain of us Catholic educators. We need to use our creativity to develop a "new humanistic synthesis" and "shape a new vision for the future" (21) that the Pope elucidated:

> Only if we are aware of our calling as individuals and as a community, to be part of God's family as his sons and daughters, will we be able to generate a new vision and muster new energy in the service of a truly integral humanism (78).

CHAPTER SEVEN

Catholic Education: Coloring Outside the Lines

· · · · · ·

Usually the main problem with life conundrums
is that we don't bring to them enough imagination.

THOMAS MOORE

· · · · · ·

B ack in mid-nineteenth century England, Queen Victoria ruled the British
Empire and yet found time to have nine children with her beloved Prince
Albert. And, as some historians tell us, Albert became the main influence over
Victoria's political views. Though they seemed to have an extremely happy
marriage, there is a story told about a particularly troubling quarrel. Albert,
distressed with the Queen over some issue, walked out on her and, as the story
goes, and locked himself in his private quarters. Victoria followed him but became frustrated because she found his door locked. She pounded on it and proclaimed in a loud voice to Albert, "Open this door; it is the Queen of England."

But the door remained locked. More pounding followed for a few mo-
ments. Then there was a deafening pause. The next sound was a gentle tap, tap,
tap. Albert inquired, "Who is there?" Then, sotto voce, Queen Victoria said,
"Albert, it is your loving wife, Vickie." Prince Albert opened the door immediately.

So it is today in Catholic education. Many are banging on its door and as-
sertively proclaiming what they think Catholic education should be: alumni
and alumnae, parents, students, former students, trustees, benefactors. However, no entity bangs harder and more insistently "proclaiming" authority

over Catholic schools than the institutional church, including individuals and groups within diocesan, archdiocesan, and curial bureaucracies. However, unlike Queen Victoria and her beloved Albert, it does not appear that the institutional church is willing to pause and gently knock in order to seek dialogue with Catholic educators—or religious educators of other faith backgrounds either—in a sensitive, open, free, and respectful manner. This is most unfortunate, since there is great wisdom to be discovered in such dialogues.

• • • • • •

The Catholic message and Gospel must be heard, understood, and lived by people who are informed and captured by their truth

• • • • • •

As a different example, given today's globally interactive world, with different societies and cultures with wildly different values, wouldn't it be out-of-place and, more importantly, ineffective, for Catholic schools and universities to bang on the doors of their students and their families and the world-at-large as if their authority as "Catholic" makes them sole dispensers of truth? Believe me, as an educator all my life, I know this will not work.

Many in the institutional church still do not fully appreciate how they should relate to Catholic education. Instead of being a truly loving and serving authority, the bishops and others behave in ways that are perceived by Catholic educators as rigid, intrusive, dogmatic, and uncaring. Church officials' insistence on proclaiming their authority over Catholic education does not enhance but rather significantly diminishes their credibility and effectiveness. Their continued insistence on controlling the message results in serious and detrimental consequences, not only for individual Catholic schools but also for the church's overall mission to the world.

The Catholic message and the Gospel of Jesus Christ are needed in this third millennium, which has begun with turmoil and terrorism in unprecedented ways. However, that message and Gospel must be heard, understood, and lived by people—especially young people—who are informed and captured by their truth, not coerced into submission. Clearly, this is no longer (if it ever was) accomplished by banging on the doors of the minds and hearts of people—claiming absolute authority, demanding definitive assent not only to the substance but the articulation of the message, and insisting on ideological acquiescence across the board on everything from the existence of God to the ordination of women.

The real truth is that the totality of divine revelation is not found in dogmas, doctrines, or dictums of institutional church leaders of any particular time. Catholics, at least, believe that revelation is found in the grace-filled presence of the Holy Spirit dwelling in the hearts and minds of the entire church when the faithful are engaged in honest dialogue not only with the institutional church but also with the world.

Let's face it: No earthly authority, not even the pope, can cause faith and zeal to become real by banging on the doors of people's hearts. The French philosopher, Maurice Merleau-Ponty, in his book, *Humanism and Terror*, said this quite well: "Whatever one's philosophical or even theological position, a society is not the temple of value-idols that figure on the front of its monuments or in its constitutional scrolls; the value of a society is the value it places upon man's relation to man."

The world has seen, read, or heard the institutional church's encyclicals, documents, and exhortations of the Christian messages and its proclamations of love and peace. It has earnestly attempted to carry these messages to every possible point on the globe. The message of a loving God who is a loving parent of all humankind has been brought to billions around the world. Yet, there are still wars, terrorism, and poverty all around this shrinking globe. Those in authority—the elected and self-appointed alike—have made great attempts to solve these kinds of world problems, but to little avail. Other organized religions, despite their good intentions, have had neither effective nor sustaining success with these issues.

In fact, as one considers the conflicts around the world, it is apparent that many of them have religious differences as their source. The culprits seem to be the ideological religious fundamentalists who are permitted to set the agenda of their entire respective faith communities. With the strong rhetoric of official pronouncements from their respective religious leaders, each claims a "monopoly on truth." This results in intolerance, misunderstanding, and suffering.

Most Catholics do not want their church to take this approach. They want a church that encourages people of all faiths and no professed faith to all to imagine a reality that is more in harmony with the wonderful values articulated by most religions, including the message and Good News of Jesus Christ.

Imagine a reality informed by Christ as a picture that can be painted by Catholic educators, if they are free to color outside the lines. "Coloring outside the lines" denotes that Catholic education must find new and creative ways to be responsive to the torturous problems that much of humankind experiences in global society.

Coloring outside the lines in Catholic schools means that there must be a renewal of what they do and how they do it. It also means the institutional church must not prevent Catholic schools from meeting their students where those students are on their faith journey—including those students, Catholic and non-Catholic alike—who are not at the same point doctrinally as the pope and bishops are. (How many people are?) Catholic school students are immersed in a culturally kaleidoscopic array of values that is colored by global diversity. The Catholic schools must be able to color outside the lines because the limits, restrictions, and controls of the traditional lines can no longer contain that new global kaleidoscope of diversity.

All Catholic educators must find the zeal it takes to prudently discard past solutions that simply do not work today. Their students no longer sit back and accept with quiet docility the authoritative pronouncements of the institutional church, as was prevalent in the not too distant past. Catholic educators must help the church make the Christian message intelligible to those who are in a very different "spiritual geography" than that which existed, not only after "The Dawning of the Age of Aquarius" but for all those now at "The Dawning of the Age of Twitter." (Even the pope is now on Twitter!) The institutional church must see that Catholic educators can help the church out of its current quandary if it allows them to teach the minds and touch the hearts of the young who have been entrusted to them by using their students' own spiritual geography, not that of the 950s or 1950s. The world simply does not exist in a spiritual geography located in some nostalgic, hierarchically dominated era from past generations.

Pressure from those who espouse the intention of recreating the Catholic Church and Catholic schools of the past is simply not relevant to the new generations of Catholics in the world today. Indeed, conservative ideologues may point to some growing interests among people, young and old alike, who are attracted to past rubrics of the church, but we have also seen a significant movement of people leaving the church because they find it hypocritical, mean-spirited, or irrelevant. This should not be! This does not have to be!

Again, another insightful observation of Merleau-Ponty may be helpful:

> The theologian will observe that human relations have a religious significance and are under God's eye. But he will not refuse to adopt them as a touchstone and, on pain of degrading religion to a daydream, he is ultimately obliged to admit that principles and inner-life are alibis the moment they cease to animate external and everyday life.

Coloring outside the lines does not change the Catholic educator's belief in the truth of the Catholic Church. Rather, it can aid students in seeing a new picture of religious significance in human relations that will "animate external life and everyday life," as Merleau-Ponty accurately observed.

The free world is no longer ruled by the power of "command," in which authority, rules, hierarchy, dogma and bureaucracy reign. Just look around. It is easy to see that in the current paradigm it is the power of gentle persuasion that is most effective in touching the hearts of people. In this emerging world, the norm for success in messaging involves diversity, pluralism, dialogue, and controversy. Indeed, control is a nostalgic relic of the past. Can anyone seriously claim that there is any place on this planet where an individual, a government, a school, or a church of any creed, finds docile acquiescence as a response to its authority? Has not the world realized yet that, just as Queen Victoria discovered, people do not necessarily open their hearts and minds because royalty is knocking?

This is exactly why the institutional church, including Pope Francis and the hierarchy, should open its mind and relational association with Catholic schools. It is the institutional church itself that should be encouraging schools to color outside the line by engaging their students in the reality of the global world of today. In the past, Catholic schools reflected the same "condition" that the church experienced. Up until the middle of the 20th century, the church and the school were places where the prevailing dynamics could be described as orderly and predictable, embracing continuity, clarity, and certainty. People and students were quite accepting of authority, whether in society, church, or school. Authority "taught" and people "learned."

• • • • • •

Catholic schools today, and certainly in the future, need "entrepreneurial leadership."

• • • • • •

Look around you today. People challenge governments, schools, and churches as never before. Even at the very core of family life, children challenge their parents in ways that were unimaginable several decades ago. Instead of those traditional attributes of society, today there is disorder, the unknown, fragmentation, confusion, and ambiguity. Neither the Catholic school nor the institutional church can continue operating as it did in the past and expect to be relevant. That past will never return, no matter how much anyone or any institution wants it to.

In the past, Catholic schools could operate and flourish quite well with "managers" and "administrators." After all, their major focus was on maintaining a system that was "maintainable" because it had order and clarity. The administrator's role was to "control" and perpetuate the existing state of the institution. However, this model will not work in the future and even today is clearly no longer manageable. Catholic schools today, and certainly in the future, need "entrepreneurial leadership." That means leaders who will seize upon opportunities; who will understand the changing needs within society; and who will not be afraid to help create a new future for its students, its own schools, and the church. Such entrepreneurial leaders will be able to color outside the lines in schools that operate successfully in a fast changing environment. Instead of controlling the present, the leader of Catholic educational institutions must innovate its future.

Catholic Schools: Attributes

In the Past	For the Future
Order	Opportunity
Predictability	Flexibility
Continuity	Variety
Clarity	Possibility
Certainty	Unknown
⋎	⋎
Process	Intuition
Systems	Initiatives
Strategic Planning	Opportunistic Planning
⋎	⋎
Managers/Administrators	Entrepreneurial Leaders
⋎	⋎
Control the Present	Innovate for the Future

The courageous acceptance of this challenge by Catholic educators will certainly result in more tension with the institutional church. But they must accept this tension and lead the way to a future that even the institutional church must come to see as necessary for its own future viability. Catholic schools need change from their past utilization of systems as their model for operating their schools to an initiative-based action model that is more responsive to the needs of their students, the church, and the world at any particular time. And they should change their past reliance on strategic planning, to a paradigm that is more realistically responsive to the incredibly fast pace of change. They must heartily engage in what I call "opportunistic planning. "

Academic institutions have traditionally depended on processes that have guided their actions in the past. For instance, there are acceptable processes that are in place that point the way for faculties to develop curricula, evaluate teacher effectiveness, respond to outside evaluation agencies, research pedagogical applications, and more. Usually, all of these processes involve incredible amounts of resources and time to follow the prescribed methods to accomplish these tasks. Clearly, continued well thought-out and careful evaluation in all these areas is essential. However, given the rapid change of cultures and new technologies in the world strongly affecting students and how they learn, it is necessary for Catholic schools to leave room for more intuitive directions to be implemented.

What I mean by "intuitive" is "quickly responsive." In every Catholic school, a fast track that permits decisions to be made that affect the classroom or school but may not be conducive to verification with traditional models of commonly accepted academic processes needs to be developed. Actually, all schools, from primary to university, need confidence in their own collegial in-tuition—encouraging faculties and staff to come together to respond to what is happening in their own school in the context of the global realities of today. Accrediting agencies must also see this and cooperate with educational institutions in new and different ways.

Opportunistic planning involves choosing paths that bring the Gospel to light in new and creative ways. It involves choosing educational innovations based on their ability to make the Gospel values meaningful and relevant to a modern world filled with the poor and marginalized who need more than pietistic exhortations to live their lives with dignity.

The need to renew and revitalize past models of operating Catholic schools is important. In place now are systems that guide how the school day is orga-nized, how the class is scheduled from the first grade student to the post-grad-uate seminar participant at a university. There should now be enough latitude within schools to permit initiative-based action models of educating, whereby the school is sensitive to and takes advantage of what is happening both inside and outside the school. For instance, if some special event or learning oppor-tunity happens outside the school, there should be the ability within the school to move beyond the confines of the classroom. This kind of initiative-based action does not mean that students must be transported "from" the school "to" the other location. Technology must be seen not only as a means of bringing the student to the world but also a way to utilize technology to bring the world to the student and into the school.

What is needed is for Catholic schools to become leaders in seizing opportunities as they arise, often unexpectedly and unpredictably. That is the world today, whether we like it or not. This reality is and will become even more prevalent when the spiritual dimension of Catholic schools is taken into account. In order to be efficacious in the religious education of their students, Catholic schools must continue to color outside the lines, using its unique paint brush of the Christian vision of the world as it should be, what Jesus called the kingdom of God "on earth as it is in heaven." The creative teaching of that message will include using everything we have available to us as Catholic educators, including our own faith and the support of both the institutional church and the entire people of God.

CHAPTER EIGHT

Catholic Schools...Up to the Task, But Are They Willing to Do It?

• • • • • •

I have been persecuted by the Church,
by those from whom I had every right to expect help.

SAINT JOHN BAPTIST DE LA SALLE
(PATRON OF TEACHERS)

• • • • • •

There is an incident recounted regarding Clarence Darrow, the great American lawyer who opposed William Jennings Bryan in the famous *Scopes Trial* in 1926 over the teaching of the theory of evolution in schools. In one of his less famous cases, Darrow had a client who was accused of biting off another man's ear in a fight. Darrow began questioning the chief witness:

"Did you see my client put Mr. Jones' ear in his mouth?"

"No, Sir," answered the witness.

"Did you see my client bite off Mr. Jones' ear?"

Again, the witness answered, "No, Sir."

"Then," thundered Darrow in the courtroom, "how can you say that my client bit Mr. Jones' ear off?"

Meekly, the witness answered, "Because I saw him spit it out!"

Are Catholic schools up to the task of responding to the needs of their students in this third millennium while still serving the church? And will they in fact rise to the occasion?

In order to answer these two multifaceted and complex challenges, we need to examine what the track record of Catholic schools has been in this regard. Perhaps the evidence does not have to be as graphic as the sight of someone spitting an ear out of his mouth, but any conclusions about the viability of Catholic schools to address the tasks I am suggesting for them must be clear and unequivocal, precisely because they are not obvious. Here are some questions that need to be answered before any conclusions can be made:

- How have Catholic schools responded in the past to the changing times and challenges that they had to endure?
- What kind of changes did they need to initiate in order to be of service to their students and to the church?
- Were those changes merely superficial "window dressing" types of strategies or were they substantive, and significant transforming directions that were successfully implemented because of courageous leadership provided by innovative Catholic educators?
- How have they helped transform the church and society in the past?
- How have they helped students and educators grow in their distinct relationship to God?
- In other words, historically how have Catholic schools authentically done their part to build the Reign of God through the transformative power of Catholic education?

To answer these types of questions, a review of the past half-century or so of American Catholic schools in action seems appropriate. General trends in our society are apparent by review of much of the literature, media, and culture of the modern era. General assumptions and values regarding the response of Catholic education to these trends can be gleaned from studying how Catholic schools changed over time. (It must be stressed that these general trends in society were by no means recognized, accepted, or addressed by all Catholic educators at the time!)

In general, Catholic schools have continuously responded to the changing times without ever apologizing for their unequivocal dedication and commitment to their Catholic identity. In fact, they have worn this Catholic badge proudly. Yet, even with this proud and strong tradition of placing their Catholic identity front and center for all to see, Catholic schools did not attract their students *only* because they had the word "Catholic" in their name as a modifying descriptor of their schools (although for the most part it didn't hurt either). Catholic primary, secondary, and university level schools flourished during these times because, yes, they were indeed Catholic—but they were so very much more. They were great schools.

To demonstrate that this is an accurate assessment, look first at the situation before World War II. Up into the 1940s, society and culture supported and nourished what has come to be called "mainstream" values. The core values that comprised this culture were part of the very nature of society and people of those times. The obligation that people felt toward their families, nation, religion, and school was best described by the word duty. Individuals had a sense of duty that was inculcated into their very existence as citizens…and as religious believers.

People in the mainstream culture understood and accepted that *sacrifice* was sometimes necessary as a consequence of their sense of duty. Institutions within society were respected and seen as necessary organs of *authority*. Whether it was the institution of the family, the government, or the church, people accepted with docility authority as a legitimate source of truth and honor. It is easy to see that within such a mainstream society, order was a value easily attained and realized.

These were the values of the mainstream students when they arrived at the steps of those schools. Catholic schools had their rules, regulations, and procedures that were quite strict and clear. In essence, the school had rules and, for the most part, the students followed them, or else they would encounter significant trouble both in school and at home!

During those years, the Catholic Church was predominantly an immigrant church. Peoples from so many various nations and cultures—Irish, Italian, German, Polish, other, mostly Europeans—arrived at the doors of the church, and were sent to the Catholic school. It was during that time that the *more* educational opportunities the Catholic school offered its students, the *more*

Americanized the immigrant faithful became. The dedicated sisters, brothers, priests, and lay teachers were there in service not only of the church, attracting many religious vocations into its service, but also to Americanize those Catholics, promoting assimilation into the nation and fostering a generation of a dynamic Catholic influence in American society.

After World War II, starting in the late 1940s and especially throughout the 1950s, the nation was exploding and bursting with incredibly new and different ideas and expectations. The onslaught of the baby boomers into the educational system began to occur and society began to change, peoples' aspirations began to change, work opportunities began to change, and eventually the church itself began to change.

But when the entire world changes, what happens to the mainstream values of duty, sacrifice, authority, and control? Surprise! They change too.

Those mainstream values that were so very accommodating to the Catholic Church, which allowed it to exercise its authority and influence on peoples' lives, suddenly had to reckon with significantly different core values. These new values were best described in terms of *individualism, creativity, progress*, and *science*.

At this time, the nation was alive not only with baby boomers but also with booming work and business opportunities. Innovation, the leading ingredient to progress, invited creativity in all areas of the American life. Individuals had never felt more empowered and convinced of their ability to control and better their own lives. This was a significant change with which the institutional church had to contend. The faithful, especially lay people, saw themselves more as action-oriented individuals who should and could create better lives for themselves here on Earth—not simply as powerless followers content to wait for the next world to straighten out any injustices that this world offered. This attitude became somewhat of a quandary for the institutional church at the time (similar to what is occurring again now), which perhaps had become more comfortable dealing with the other-worldly aspirations of its followers.

Who came to the rescue of the church to help unravel that quandary? Yes, it was the Catholic schools. During these times (from the 1950s through the 1960s, in response to and in conjunction with the Second Vatican Council),

Catholic schools adjusted their approaches and responded to their students' new needs. Catholic educators observed that the students entering their institutions were evolving into a more significantly this-world mentality and spirituality. Catholic schools still had rules and Catholic educators saw that, at a minimum, their students tried to respect those rules. However, gone was the docile acquiescence of the previous decades. Catholic educators had to adapt to a changing, more engaged student body.

Catholic educators had to adapt to a changing, more engaged student body.

Students desired and needed preparation for a world that tied their success intimately to the knowledge they were learning in literature, mathematics, science, and—yes—religion class. Education was the *sine qua non* ingredient in the employability of the American workforce, the business world, and the professions. Catholic schools went from primarily Americanizing their first-and-second-generation immigrant students to being, so to speak, an employment agency preparing their third-and-fourth-generation students to be viable players in a land of new opportunity. At the same time, they struggled to adapt to new immigrants from Latin America and elsewhere. Once again, Catholic schools served the church and their students while doing an excellent job at being Catholic and *more!*

From the early 1970s through the 1980s, another societal transition occurred with the introduction of the Gen-Xers. The Catholic school and society at large once again went through another significant change of values and behaviors in their students. For the most part, students' former focus on individualism, creativity, progress, and science evolved into a culture where students could better be described as *skeptical, adaptable,* and *pragmatic.*

These became difficult times for families, schools, and the church in their relationship with young people. (I know, I was president of a Catholic university during those years.) There was a pervasive culture of drug use and a societal move toward permissiveness of all kinds that made it difficult to set parameters on peoples' behavior. The schools' rules and expected behaviors were constantly challenged by students.

The church met with great resistance during these times, and began to be perceived as irrelevant in the real world of freedoms of lifestyles, sexual mores, and general permissiveness in interactions between people and institutions. Once again, though, Catholic schools adapted to this changing environment and tried to play a role nearly equated to a *protective custodian* of its students by attempting to provide them with a drug-free environment. And the Catholic schools responded to these difficult challenges with significant success. They continued to teach their students and hold on to those fragile strings that were still there in their students' hearts, connecting them to the church. Granted, the relationship was quite fragile, but once again, Catholic schools served the church and their students while doing an excellent job at being Catholic and *more*!

Then came Gen-Y and the Millennials. Now Catholic schools made rules and the students would think, "What are rules?" It is not difficult to understand their reaction. After all, look at the past few decades in which they had grown up. Whom did society give them to trust? Who were the rule makers?

- *Politicians?* No one has to create a list of those politicians who have betrayed the trust of the American people by their illegal, unethical, or immoral actions. Whether they were "tap dancing in public bathrooms," stashing cash in their home freezer, not paying their taxes, or flying to their paramours on the taxpayers' dime, they were not models of propriety.
- *Sports heroes?* Many of the top players in almost all sports broke long-standing sports records while they used steroids or other drugs, or acted without any moral bearing in their lives when they got off the field or golf course.
- *Business leaders?* It wasn't just con artists like Bernie Madoff and the guys at Enron who failed us, it was the "legitimate" bankers and investors and their supposed government overseers who managed to bring the entire world financial system to its knees based on the simple act of encouraging people to borrow money they could not repay.

- *Church leaders?* Perhaps the most devastating horrors perpetrated on all of today's youth came from the institutional church itself: the sexual abuse scandals and the almost universal mishandling and sometimes actual cover-up of them. How are young people supposed to have faith in their church when its leaders have behaved so badly?

What could Catholic schools possibly have to offer their students concerning trust when this has been what is going on in both church and society? The answer is really quite simple: We must continue to teach as Jesus did. Catholic schools have clearly demonstrated over the last 50-75 years that they have been up to the task of adapting to the needs of their students while remaining faithful and serving the church. They need to keep doing so.

• • • • • •

Excellence in Catholic education will be measured by how Catholic schools allow and encourage their students to trust them and, eventually, to once again trust the institutional church.

• • • • • •

Now, the second part of this query: "but will they?" Will Catholic schools continue to adapt to the new and changing needs of its students and simultaneously help the church recover its deteriorated reputation?

On second thought, perhaps this is not the precise question. The question should be, "Will the institutional church let them?" This seems to be the fair and appropriate question when we take into consideration that for Catholic schools to respond to their students' needs today they must transform how they embrace and teach excellence in today's world. This effort, if done correctly, could elicit continued and significant intrusions into Catholic schools by the institutional church. In fact, we have already seen plenty of this.

Excellence in Catholic education will be measured now and in the future by how Catholic schools allow and encourage their students to trust them and, eventually, to once again trust the institutional church. Excellence in Catholic education demands that Catholic educators accept, love, and teach their students wherever they are on *their* spiritual journey. We must not try to mold our students into some rigid, preconceived form acceptable to the institutional church leaders, with ourselves seen as *gate-keepers* instead of *door openers*.

Do not expect young people to acquiesce with docility if all that Catholic educators can give them are pious exhortations and formulaic catechetical answers to their questions. Catholic educational institutions must accompany their students on their journey toward the magnificent Christian mystery of the Word made Flesh. But that journey must contain a road map that includes more signs than just what is provided by doctrinal and rote formulas directing the inquisitive to a prescribed destination.

Trust in Catholic schools, or for that matter trust in the institutional church or the church itself, should have very little to do with power, control, or domination—certainly not today, if it ever did. Building trust in contemporary society has everything to do with affirming and empowering, not demanding or compelling. If youth do not have trust in their Catholic schools to accompany them *unconditionally* on their faith journey, how can they believe that the Holy Spirit can or will do so?

Without this trust, as you have probably heard it said, the problem is not that our youth will believe in nothing. The problem is that they will believe in *anything*.

Excellence in Catholic education should be—no, it must be—measured to the degree that students will have trust in Catholic educators personally and in their schools and universities to have their best interests at heart. Excellence in the future will be measured by the degree to which there is faithful, candid and courageous, open and constructive questioning of the institutional church, without rancor or mean-spiritedness. Such an attitude is not disloyal to the church or to the Catholic educational heritage.

The hierarchy should see in this picture of youth today an evolving new theology of obedience not through submission and docility to a relationship of loving accompaniment on their journey through exploration, dialogue, response, questioning, and seeing others in their lived reality. Catholic educators can help the bishops learn how to do this, if they will let them. This will not make the church, the school, or the students any less Catholic; it will make them *truly* Catholic.

Part Two

• • • • • •

Dynamics Needed
for the Transformation
of Catholic Schools

• • • • • •

DYNAMIC ONE

Risk and Invent

• • • • • •

Love is a restraint of power; I could but I will not.
I could come down from the cross but I will not.
We have to learn the restraint of power.

Rev. Otis Moss III

• • • • • •

Nations, governments, world organizations, foundations, educational institutions, and religions all around the globe strive to make this a better and more peaceful world, a world in which people have a reasonable possibility of living with human dignity. These efforts can be realized in institutions regardless of whether they are secularly orientated or religiously motivated. The most essential ingredient in any of these efforts is this: there must be people of good will who are committed to the principle that the sisterhood and brotherhood of all humanity transcends any nation, any culture, or any affinity group's respective beliefs.

However, even with such a strong humanistic desire for unity within diversity, history has taught us all a lesson: Desire for peace and prosperity is not enough! Certainly desire, which we might also call "wishful thinking," has not yet prevented wars, clashes between classes, poverty, and terrorism.

There are many people of good will who have not yet accepted the dynamics needed to actually implement their desire for unity among all peoples of the world. This is where the Catholic Church and Catholic educational institutions can play a vital role and become a model for the paradigm shift that is desperately needed.

Michel Sauvage, FSC, a De LaSalle Christian Brother and accomplished theologian, made a keen observation that may be helpful in understanding the unique role that Christians can play in this regard:

[That] hope invites us to fully engage in God's "today," attentive to situations and calls, close to all, open to sharing and to pluralism. That, in ourselves and among our brothers and sisters, every day, the Spirit is creator, and that it is more vital and more faithful "to take care not to extinguish the Spirit" than to cling to what seems to guarantee in advance the straightness of the road and the consistency of the pace of those on the journey. That, in this journey, step-by-step, the Spirit who "possesses us and whom we possess," is still diffusing in our hearts the love of Christ, in whose footsteps we continue to move onwards. And that this same Holy Spirit educates us day after day to abandon ourselves to a Father who, both in the depths of ourselves and through the most mundane or the most unexpected events, never ceases to call us to begin again, to go out, to risk, to invent.

To risk and to invent are difficult enough for individuals, but they are significantly more complex for institutions. The dynamics required to accomplish this creativity are engendered, fostered, and nourished in the church because the Holy Spirit is present. Our faith ensures this. Therefore, the church is uniquely qualified to model for the world those qualities that make it possible to be a "light to the world." But it is not enough for the church only to *talk* about the Gospel and *proclaim* pietistic exhortations if it is to be a model for the world. It must *risk* its traditional ways of doing things for the past two thousand years and *invent* new and relevant ways that respond to today's world needs.

The institutional church must remind itself of the more inclusive and fuller appreciation of God's revelation to us that Vatican II brought to the understanding of *tradition* in the church. An important contributor to this expansive insight into tradition was the French Dominican priest, Yves Congar, especially as elaborated in his book *Tradition and Traditions*. Congar pointed to the church's tradition as an historical process by which it presents the mystery of

Christ in a vibrant and relevant way for the particular times. For Congar, tradition is not some rote, immutable "sameness;" rather it is a living and active dynamic in every age.

Everyone in the church—the institutional leaders, Catholic educators, and the entire People of God—must remind themselves of this very point as it was also expressed in 2 Corinthians: "For anyone who is in Christ, there is a new creation, everything old has passed away; see, everything has become new."

Renewal is not enough. Change is not enough. Simply buffing and polishing the old will not do the job. The call is for an entirely "new creation" that never existed before. The call is for *transformation*. Transformation is considerably more challenging than renewal, because transformation involves doing what has never before been done or even pondered. Truly it means a *new creation*, not continuity or even a renewal of past practices.

• • • • • •

Transformation means a new creation, not continuity or even a renewal of past practices.

• • • • • •

The institutional church is called to have faith in itself and its schools and the People of God in ways that will give rise to the zeal to do things that have never even been thought of before. This kind of attitude is what will make it possible to unravel the quandary the church is in today: how to restore its relevance, respect, and authority.

The greatest risk this transformation presents is that the usual institutional *modus operandi* will no longer apply to the future that is being created now, whether the hierarchy likes it or not. Those who are in the established power base within the church can never easily accept such flux. Reliance on traditional procedures, customs, and rules in the church no longer can assure the previously expected outcomes. Uncertainty and unpredictability have been introduced into the total institutional environment.

To be responsive to the new problems of a new world, the institutional church must take appropriate risks in order to invent a new and creative existence which will speak to a world which is itself inventing new ways of acting.

It is unfortunate that many of the worldly change agents are not bringing about a future of beauty, dignity, and peace. Instead there is growing marginalization, degradation, and terrorism. So the urgency for Gospel-values-based transformation is not only necessary for the church and its own future—such urgency is needed for the future of a world.

The Gospel calls for those who live in Christ to acknowledge "everything old has passed away." There is need for a "new creation." This is not just some beautiful metaphor that suggests that Christians need only to rearrange and make superficial changes in themselves and the world and that after we die everything will be perfect. At the core of the Christian soul is a genuine this-worldly sensibility arising from the dynamic to invent a future where Christ's love truly reigns in the here and now. The Christian is not called to *react* to today's circumstances and reality. Rather the Christian is called to create the future in spite of today's realities. And there is a simple fact that must be recognized: We cannot create something new without taking a *risk*. The institutional church must encourage and support this *dynamic of risk* and invent a paradigm of a Gospel-values-imbued future for this world through its faith in the Holy Spirit, who enkindles in the faithful the fire of God's love. And who is better designed and positioned to do this than Catholic schools?

Through its own transformation, the Catholic school can become a leader for the transformation of the entire world population to live in peace and dignity. There is a need to harness the power of the Spirit already working in the hearts of the faithful. The task is very great and comes with great risk. But heed the admonition of Pope John Paul II as he opened the Lenten season on March 5, 2003, against the backdrop of the war with Iraq: "There won't be peace on Earth as long as oppression of people, social injustices, and economic imbalances exist.... A widespread conversion of hearts to love is needed."

This kind of dynamic is not some outlandish or unrealistic expectation. But it does mean that Catholic schools must not be afraid to risk making drastic changes to how they presently operate. The church's Tradition must not be used as the high walls that currently shield the institutional church from the spiritual power of all those on the other side of those walls. Catholic schools should teach that Tradition, properly understood, is a living, breathing reality that allows for God's revelation to continue as a vibrant force in the present and the future. For the Catholic schools to help the institutional church unravel its present quandary, they must help their students spiritually "knock down those walls."

Indeed, that is a risk. But a "new creation" is ready to be invented. A new future awaits us all once those walls are knocked down. It is a kind of future that the great theologian Karl Rahner described when he so beautifully wrote:

> The real future is the one that comes in its own time and often leaves our predictions and plans in shreds. What is perhaps most difficult as a way of living in preparation for the real future is letting go of something beautiful which we ourselves have helped to create. It may be relinquished, not because it has lost its beauty, but because the time has passed. Some other new beauty is being made.

This is the clear mandate for Catholic education that will facilitate its vital role of helping Christianity go beyond the story of its past and create a new story. With this spirit, the church can begin to bring people together in this new globalized society.

So with this as a background, the first dynamic needed for the transformation of Catholic schools may be stated in this way:

DYNAMIC ONE
Treasure Tradition, properly understood.
Try transition.
Trust in transformation!

DYNAMIC TWO

Develop Your Style

• • • • • •

God make me the person that my dog thinks I am.

<small>ANONYMOUS</small>

• • • • • •

An Italian colleague in Rome is a knowledgeable aficionado of all types of art. One day, after explaining to him my great appreciation for the Renaissance masters, I told him that I especially admired the works of Giotto di Bondone (1267–1337). Giotto, as he is commonly known, was considered the prime mover in the beginnings of Italian Renaissance art. Instead of the expected flat and one-dimensional art that preceded him, Giotto used new techniques that brought a vibrant, real-life quality to his works.

Giotto was an innovator who introduced spatial perspective and a unity of surroundings and figures to his paintings. He gave expression to the faces of the people in his paintings that made the viewer see attitude and emotion more vividly. In essence, Giotto transformed the art world because his paintings introduced a more natural and true three-dimensional representation of real life.

"Not so," said my Italian colleague to my mini-art lesson. "It is true that Giotto developed a more realistic representation than previously seen in the art world." But then he asked, "Is the real world that you live in understandable in just three dimensions?"

I reflected on my friend's question, with an answer arising quickly and clearly to my brain: Indeed, to understand people, events, politics, economics, history, sociology, religion—to understand the world—clearly takes much more than three dimensions. In fact, there is no finite number of dimensions that could possibly comprehend the totality of the mystery of life itself, or even of an individual person.

Then my insightful colleague brought another possibility to my attention. Perhaps, he said, I should try to better understand the works of the Spaniard Pablo Picasso (1881–1973) since *he* depicted reality more clearly than Giotto! This was an astonishing comment, since anyone with even a cursory overview of his art would not be likely to describe Picasso's work as realistic. A simple quick review of Picasso's works reveals the incredibly drastic and changing techniques the artist used, which transformed the art world every bit as much as Giotto had, but through the use of blatantly unique perspectives. Picasso became known for the periods that represented his works: the Blue Period, the Rose Period, the African-Influenced Period, the Modernist Period, the Surrealism Period, the Cubist Period, etc. He did not limit himself to three dimensions, even though most of his art was done on flat canvases.

Though many still describe Picasso's work as "bizarre," the fact is that for him the reality of life is not expressed simply in dimensions seen only with a person's physical eyes. The reality of life—the mystery of life—is multidimensional and is, therefore, better captured in art that calls upon the viewers to see also with their minds' eye (or, can we say, soul).

Picasso attempted to explore reality in its totality and mystery, and in doing so he created new ways to represent life. He used complexity and techniques rarely imagined before in the art world: using perspectives from behind, on top, inside, and within and without the scene and/or person he was depicting. Seemingly miraculously, he did all of this at the same time in the same piece of artwork!

Consistent with his approach, Picasso once observed:

God is just another artist. He made a giraffe, an elephant, and a cat. He has no style. He just keeps trying new things.

It seems to me that this dynamic of developing your own style is certainly needed in today's fast-changing-technologically-rampant-world: Keep trying new things using different perspectives. God does! This development of style is a dynamic not only for nations and societies, but also for Catholic schools. Of course, I do not mean to imply that change for the sake of change is good. Rather, the necessity for change is demanded by the reality of the incredible amounts of new knowledge and information that are exploding as a result of new scientific and human research coming to the world at a faster and faster pace.

It is within the spirit of tradition, properly understood, that truth can be discovered. Tradition, the lived experience of the faithful, is what allows change to happen. It must be emphasized that people in today's world are on a journey that probably Giotto could not paint very well. Perhaps Catholic schools can create a new tapestry that will depict a future more in the style of a Picasso painting: creative, innovative, with not too much conformity to the ordinary but with much imagination grasping beauty in the diversity and expansiveness of Christ's love for all. This style will emphasize a continuity with love—not the past.

. . . . . .

Tradition, the lived experience of the faithful, is what allows change to happen.

. . . . . .

It is time for Catholic schools to help create that brilliant tapestry, which will lead the world to see and embrace a new and understandable path to the Christian ideal of holiness. Certainly, though, this new tapestry will have different colors, lines, and perspectives from those societal dynamics encountered by the Christians from two thousand years ago. It is time to re-focus, renew, and recreate the traditional mission and methods of operation of Catholic schools in order to find better and more immediately relevant ways to serve people.

When any institution is in this transitional stage, and there is a conscious realization that transformation is needed, it is not the time when a style that insists on rules, rubrics, and orthodoxy will be especially meaningful or effective. In times of innovation and creativity, actions are more multidimensional in scope and, as such, order and predictability often include some confusion and uncertainty. The painting of transformation will always be more like a Picasso than a Giotto painting.

Currently, there are many theologians and faithful Catholics from all professions, lifestyles, and walks-of-life who are primed and ready to try new things that can help the institutional church to unravel its current quandary. However, they are met with hierarchically placed roadblocks that either discredit the individual or resort to an assertion of authority to prevent dialogue and experimentation on different ways to view a particular topic.

Franciscan priest Richard Rohr has contributed much in developing and exploring new ways to theologize that speak more understandably and meaningfully to people. He insightfully points out that people today have a different consciousness in their understanding of the Gospel message, a new spiritual geography. In essence, the new generations of those influenced by globalized society may appreciate Giotto's masterpieces, but they see their church's reality with a Picasso-like perspective that is qualitatively far removed from how the hierarchy, as the institutional force, seeks to paint its traditional picture of reality.

For example, in his presentation of theology Rohr explains that another word for contemplation is "non-dualistic thinking." His is not a theology of either/or and us/them. It is a theology that has much more than a singular focus and preoccupation with issues such as abortion, condom use, and gay marriage. It is a theology based on the vision of peace and justice central to the ministry of Jesus. It is a theology that helps build community with a vision that is complementary to—not in competition with—the institutional church. Yet institutional church leaders do not encourage pursuing this new way of thinking, since they probably see it as competing with their control and authority.

Another startling situation was made public in November 2010, at the Don Bosco Catholic parish in suburban Brussels. Since there is a severe shortage of priests there, a lay parishioner, Willy Delsaert, performs a Sunday ritual in which bread and wine is shared with the community present. This is not uncommon in this Flemish-speaking region of Belgium. It is estimated that there are currently about a dozen of these alternative Catholic communities, and the number is quickly growing.

Of course this practice is not in conformity with Vatican orthodoxy, and the official Belgium church tries to keep its distance from this movement. The purpose of noting it here is neither to condone nor attempt to legitimize the canonical orthodoxy of this practice. Rather, the point is to observe that institutional church leaders do not respect the efforts of lay people trying new things in order to serve and worship God. Instead, at best, they ignore such efforts, and point out the lack of canonical validity.

The faithful clearly see that, because so much has changed in the church, they are hindered in their access to the sacraments and their worship of God. Instead of taking the leadership role, being creative, and trying new things, institutional church leaders resort to traditional orthodoxy—a "hermeneutic of continuity" they now call it—that no longer supplies solutions. If this lack of support continues, more and more of the faithful will try new things, without institutional approval or participation, in order to praise and worship in this new world where the faithful realize that the church can no longer function as it traditionally has.

The appropriate opportunity for Catholic schools to guide and influence the transformation that is taking place in the church and in the world is *now*. The opportunity, impulse, and inspiration to try new things that respond to new needs will not be placed on hold until people adapt to the "style" and pace of change that the hierarchy desires. Catholic schools can and must fill this vacuum.

Naomi Shihab Nye, the award-winning American poet born of a Palestinian father and American mother, wrote the poem, *Missing the Boat*, capturing the sense of opportunity missed:

It is not so much that the boat passed
and you failed to notice it.
It is more like the boat stopping
directly outside your bedroom window,
the captain blowing the signal horn,
the band playing the rousing march.
The boat shouted, waving bright flags,
its silver hull blinding in the sunlight.
But you had this idea you were going by train.
You kept checking the time-tables,

digging for tracks.
And the boat got tired of you,
So tired it pulled up the anchor
and raised the ramp.
The boat bobbed into the distance
shrinking like a toy—
at which point you probably realized
you had always loved the sea.

A first read of Nye's poem gives the impression that its message was tailor-made for the Catholic Church's benefit. This poem should be required reading for all Catholic educators. The opportunity to take Christ's message to the world today requires trying new things and having the faith to get on that boat that is surely heading to the future. Many good and faithful people are convinced that the captain of that boat is none other than the Holy Spirit "waving bright flags," as all see "its silver hull blinding in the sunlight."

The boat will not wait too much longer! Who will get on that boat?

With this image in mind the second dynamic needed for the transformation of Catholic schools is:

DYNAMIC TWO
Don't worry about style.
God doesn't.
Try new things now!

DYNAMIC THREE

Paradigm This and Imagine That

• • • • • •

Unfurl the sails, and let God steer us where he will.

Saint Bede

• • • • • •

In today's diverse and pluralistic world, popular jargon speaks with much repetition about the significant roles that what are called "paradigms" play in the understanding of inter-personal and inter-cultural dynamics. Paradigms are those models and frameworks of thought imposed by the predominant culture and imbedded in the human mind. They are, in effect, schemes for understanding and explaining aspects of the experienced reality. They give form to how individuals actually view the world. Simply stated, different cultures cause people to accept and/or speak about their experiences in different ways.

Most of us do not recognize the very paradigms we operate under. Part of the job of education, especially Catholic education, is to make sure that students do become aware of their own paradigms and those of others. Christianity, and more specifically Catholicism, is one such paradigm, although even that paradigm has multiple versions and nuances.

The role of paradigms in human society amid global diversity is a significant factor as this world strives to live in peace and harmony on a shrinking world of competing values. The most extreme and dramatic result of opposing paradigms occurs when people act violently as a response to their religion's perceived command while the recipients of that violence sees it as an evil act of terrorism. Throughout history, religion is one of the usual suspects in severe paradigm clashes.

The research of Marilyn Ferguson in her book *The Aquarian Conspiracy*, was a significant contribution to the intellectual understanding of the role of paradigms and how they affect knowledge. In the world of research, in its most basic element, scientists observe reality through the accumulation of observable facts. That is to say that the Western paradigm seeking to understand reality is dependent on accumulating and observing data, information, statistics, etc. This model of seeing reality in a factual way can be traced back to 18th-century Europe's Age of Enlightenment and extended from then to the paradigm described as Scientific Positivism.

This paradigm is appropriate if you are immersed in the Westernized world that accepts this framework of thought as a way—or the only way—to comprehend reality. However, problems arise when diversity abounds and competing paradigms flourish and are in constant contact because of instantaneous communications and ease of travel.

Can anyone today be sure of *any* facts? In fact, do facts still exist? "That is absurd," you might say, "facts are what they are. There is no arguing about them." Well, consider this. Clifford Geertz, an influential anthropologist, studied the phenomenon called "facts." He observed and studied facts related to the influence of cultural clashes such as those regarding religious fundamentalism. In his book *After the Fact*, he suggests that in this "post-structuralist," "post-modernist," "post-humanist" age, there is no longer one prevailing standard (paradigm) for judging what the facts are, nor even what a fact is! If this is true, then relativism seems to take on even more power. Is this the death of scientific truth? Or does this at least compel us all to be in open and careful dialogue in order to understand the facts as perceived by others?

To seek some insights into these conundrums, observe Pope John Paul II's statement in *Centesimus Annus* (#24): "At the heart of every culture lies the attitude a person takes to the greatest mystery, the mystery of God." This does not mean that Christians strive for a culture that regresses to some nostalgic medieval theocracy. Rather, as Michael Paul Gallagher, a Jesuit theology professor at Rome's Gregorian University, powerfully demonstrates in his book *Clash-*

ing Symbols, Christian evangelization needs balancing by developing a sense of the plurality of cultures. Though the Gospel message should be understood as independent of specific cultures, Christianity, like all religions, must be lived by people within their cultural realities and with the facts as they understand them.

Therefore, for Catholic schools the proper response to the existence of paradigms lies in teaching students to be able to enter a culture without becoming subject to that culture in a way that would diminish Gospel values. The Catholic school cannot prepare its students for this kind of world if it continues to insist and speak about its doctrine, theology, and spirituality in a rigid, predetermined, Western-biased, and univocal manner.

The question rightfully arises, then: What dynamic and quality is needed by Catholic educators in order to speak and be understood in this third millennium world, without becoming relativists? It may be helpful in finding an answer by referring to Toni Morrison's beautiful novel, *Beloved*.

• • • • • •

Christianity, like all religions, must be lived by people within their cultural realities and with the facts as they understand them.

• • • • • •

In this book, Morrison tells the story of an African-American slave woman, a preacher named Baby Suggs. Preacher Suggs would clandestinely take her "congregation" of slaves on Saturday afternoons to an open field far out in the nearby woods. It was here that Baby Suggs would preach to her followers in her own open-air cathedral. At times they would be laughing or dancing and sometimes crying. During these gatherings, she would not tell her congregation of sin, suffering, and eternal damnation. They were living in hell on Earth. They already knew what suffering was. They were condemned by the sin of slavery.

However, each week Baby Suggs would preach to those slaves: "The only grace you could have is the grace that you can imagine. If you do not see it, you will not have it!"

Imagination, indeed, is probably the most blessed grace that a person of faith can have. We believe it was God the Creator who *imagined* every single thing and person into existence. It was God who "saw" a world, a universe, a cosmos and then brought it into existence and sustains it now.

Perhaps, when Scripture talks of us humans as being made "in the image and likeness of God," it may be the ability to *imagine* that primarily makes us so. (It certainly isn't our looks!)

Imagination is what helps people and institutions acknowledge their own paradigms and those of others. It allows us to dream of things that are not there now but could become reality if we could work together to make them happen. Here is the obvious dynamic that Catholic schools must embrace: Just because imagination helps us see things that are not apparent, it is not the enemy of religion or, specifically Christianity, or even more specifically Catholicism. Rather imagination is what helps us reinterpret Catholic teachings, practices, and history in new and meaningful ways that are understandable to young people in today's world. Creative use of the imagination dynamic will allow us all to perceive new knowledge that can further unfold God's mystery of life and love on this Earth. With imaginative and creative teaching, Catholic schools will be better able to unfold Christian values for students in ways that are not always attainable in the world of scientific positivism and religious dogmatism.

The world today, with its multiple webs of interactions, cultural diversity, complexity, and interdependence, requires a new imagination that will help students see, think, and solve problems in different ways. Unleashing this power of the imagination in our students is essential for Catholic education and its future viability. No longer are the Western intellectual traditions the only ways to approach knowledge, whether in science, philosophy, or theology. The Western bias toward rational, scientific, direct, dualistic, and linear approaches to reality do not necessarily encompass all contemporary patterns of thought. Our students need to know this.

There has come into this diverse world a process that approaches reality from all dimensions and at many levels. Linda J. Sheplace, in her book, *Lifting the Veil: The Feminine Face of Science*, has described this process as "fuzzy logic." There is a marvelous entitlement for Catholic schools in this concept, which can be helpful if it helps open up our students' imaginations to new ways of thinking. The old Judy Collins song says, "I've looked at life from both sides now." But today two is not enough. How many sides are there to each issue, to each problem? How many ways are there to teach science, philosophy, religion, etc.? How many ways are there to understand the infinite mystery of God? How many ways are there to understand what Jesus of Nazareth had in mind for his vision of the kingdom of God "on earth as it is in heaven"?

Acceptance of this expansive and imaginative new way of seeing reality allows for greater truth to unfold, for more penetrating mental explorations, and for developing alternative scenarios that can bring about action leading to desired changes in both society and church. No doubt this type of creativity, which fosters exploration and opening up the imagination, is problematic to authoritative institutions, including the institutional church.

Catholic schools can help the institutional church overcome this quandary by leading the way. However, the hierarchy must admit that Jesus Christ is Savior to all peoples of the world—not just those who think like the Catholic hierarchy, pray with Catholic rubrics, or believe exactly as they do. As Fernando Miguens so poignantly observes in his book, *Fe y Cultura en la Ensenanza de Juan Pablo II*, there can be no single Christian culture; rather there are many different cultures to be "Christianized." He cautions that no one should identify "universalization" as "uniformity."

It is imperative for us Catholics to make the universal Christ understood in a church that often is seen by many to favor just one culture, one paradigm, and one historical context: the Western (really the Roman) tradition. The Catholic schools can help us do that.

The insightful theologian, Walter Ong, SJ, approached this same idea from another viewpoint. He observed that the term *Catholic* is a Greek-based term, said to mean universal; but is not based on the Latin *universalis*. The distinction is that the Greek term *Katholika* contains *holos,* meaning "through, within, without, up and down." Thus, *Katholika* refers to the whole with no constricting or limiting factors. The Latin *universalis* also means "universal" but implies being contained by defined borders, which is a much more limiting context.

Perhaps the early church fathers thought the borders of the Catholic Church should be movable and expansive as they went out "to teach all nations." But they also imagined a more diverse and varied world in which all need Jesus Christ.

As Walter Ong so clearly stated:

> To deal with "catholicity" or globalization and its implications, we must be intimately aware so far as possible of the whole cosmos in which our globe is situated. The globe on which we live is part of God's creation. Christian faith must include what we now know of the size and age of God's creation. It is suicidal not to take account of this knowledge, to talk and act as though it were not there.

And so follows the third dynamic needed for transformation of our Catholic schools:

DYNAMIC THREE
Recognize paradigms, your own and that of others.
If you cannot see it, you will never have it.
Imagine that!

DYNAMIC FOUR

See What Might Be Otherwise

• • • • • •

When any government, or church for that matter, undertakes to say to its subjects, "This you may not read, this you may not see, this is forbidden to know," the end result is tyranny and oppression, no matter how holy the motives.

ROBERT A. HEINLEIN

• • • • • •

At the opening of William Shakespeare's *Julius Caesar*, Cassius and Brutus are together after Marc Antony's entourage has just passed by. In Act I, Scene 2, Cassius, the "sly one," peers into the eyes of Brutus the "good one," and asks him a peculiar question.

He leans into Brutus and asks, "Can you see your face?" Startled, Brutus replies, "No, Cassius, for the eye sees not itself but by reflection, by some other thing." Then immediately Cassius says to Brutus:

'Tis just, therefore, be prepared to hear. And since you know you cannot see so well as by reflection, I, your glass, will modestly discover to yourself, that of yourself of which you yet know not of.

And thus is the beginning of the turning of Brutus, "a good man," into one of the intriguers and assassins of Caesar. The sly Cassius knew only too well that if he became Brutus' "glass" (mirror) and prevented him from seeing the total reality of the situation, then he could move even a good man to do his evil biddings.

It is always a dangerous situation for persons or groups to be so closed in upon themselves that all they have available to "see reality" is their own image or that of the group to which they belong. It would have been better for Brutus (certainly for Caesar) if Cassius had offered to open windows around Brutus instead of giving him a mirror! But, then, Cassius' plot would not have been successful if Brutus was permitted to see the full picture of the real circumstances and evil values surrounding the horrible deed that was to take place.

The importance of nurturing and associating with goodness and with others is a healthy and wholesome dynamic that fosters the development of an integrated personality. Whether spiritually, psychologically, or socially, individuals do not experience healthy growth and development if they are continually closed in upon themselves or only in contact with others who think and act exactly as they do. No one person (not even the new Pope Francis) nor any closed-minded group (the institutional church) can be a good enough "mirror" to reflect all the splendor of the diversity of God's creation. Even though it is clearly more comfortable and easier to interact with like-minded people, to do so turns human development toward self-centeredness and narrow mindedness. Certainly, in humanistic terms, no one should be permitted to have only a Cassius as a "mirror" into which the full potential of human possibilities can be seen. It takes open windows, not looking into mirrors, to see the potential of humanity and the mystery of God in its fullest glory.

It takes open windows to see the potential of humanity and the mystery of God in its fullest glory.

With the use of some imagination, for Catholic schools there may be a corollary to Shakespeare's *Julius Caesar* and the development of the person as a spiritual being. This could be seen in the Old Testament story of Jonah. The Lord commanded Jonah, "Go at once to Nineveh, that great city, and cry out against it, for their wickedness has come up before me" (Jonah 1:1). Historically, Jonah and his people did not want anything to do with Nineveh, since these wicked people were despised by the good, righteous, Lord-fearing Hebrews such as Jonah. Yet the Lord commanded him to go and save these outcasts from destruction.

Surprisingly, Jonah refused this command and ran away from the Lord, taking a ship to Tarshish. On the sea, the Lord sent a violent storm and the boat was in danger of sinking. Jonah was thrown overboard by the crew in order to appease God, who they knew had sent that storm to punish the prophet. However, the Lord immediately sent a huge fish to save Jonah by swallowing him. Then, this fish vomited Jonah onto dry land. With Jonah now saved from drowning, the Lord, for the second time, commanded him to go to the dreaded city of Nineveh to convert them from their wickedness.

Only then did Jonah reluctantly go there and, with his preaching, exhorted the people of Nineveh to change their sinful ways. They did change and were then saved by the Lord from destruction. However, as the story goes, instead of being grateful Jonah is angry with the Lord because he was so compassionate to those sinners. In essence Jonah was feeling that it was *he* who was the righteous one doing the Lord's work and yet the Lord was compassionate to the sinners.

Many who follow the rubrics and details of religious "laws and regulations" look into the mirror and see themselves as the righteous and the pure—better than those "others." Their reluctance and fears elicit only half-hearted responses from most people to the invitation of the God who loves all unconditionally: the stranger, the foreigner, the sinner, the wicked, the disordered, the nonbeliever. God had to ask Jonah twice, and still the prophet was reluctant. And then Jonah had the audacity to be angry with God for showing compassion for the wicked people of Nineveh.

In both the Shakespeare and the biblical stories, albeit with different imagery, the focal point is on the need for the individual person to appreciate that the world is more than a narrow and closed-in reality that involves only the "me" and the "us." These are the very dynamics that are needed in Catholic schools to kindle the hearts of all the faithful. The church enters this third millennium on a shrinking globe that is bringing forth more diversity than the world has ever experienced. Leadership is sorely needed that will light the way to help the faithful see that the Lord is calling the church today to go to the people of today's Nineveh!

The church teaches and celebrates Pentecost as the "birthday" of the church here on Earth. However, what it seems to forget is that the coming of the Holy

Spirit in the church on Pentecost may symbolize more than a birthday. Perhaps the more striking message is that the Lord wanted to help his new church to listen and understand people—all people—even those whom the institutional church does not see when it looks into its own mirrors: those who are different; those who think or believe differently; those with different lifestyles; those in need of God's grace and unconditional love, even if they don't yet know it.

There are two directions those of us in Catholic education can pursue. We can succumb to inappropriate pressures to look into the institutional church's mirror and be forced to accept that its position is the only correct one, or we can go to Nineveh, as the Holy Spirit seems to be calling us, and see that we need to open some of our windows and look out at the world as it really is. Catholic schools must change, not because we should succumb to popular pressure but rather because we need to revise our methods and curriculum to recognize and incorporate into our teaching new scientific insights and knowledge. We must accompany our students where they are on their spiritual journey—and at times we will need courage to do that.

This willingness to be open to transformation has been captured in a beautiful insight, expressed by Maxine Greene in her article, "Aesthetic Literacy In General Education" (The National Society of the Study of Education, Philosophy and Education, Chicago, 1981):

> To break with ordinariness and stock response is, at any age, to achieve a new readiness, a new ripeness. Not only will there be awareness of things in their particularity, of beauty and variety and form. There will be a fresh orientation to the search for meaning in the many spheres of life.

> ... People may be brought to watch and to listen with increasing wide-awakeness, attentiveness, and care. And they may be brought to discover multiple ways of looking at blackbirds and whales and riverbanks and city streets, looking at things as if they might be otherwise than they are.

With the guidance of the Holy Spirit, which we are confident is with us always, we Catholic educators can lead the People of God to "a fresh orientation to the search for meaning" in the church. But we must first realize that we must look at how we "might be otherwise" than we are in order to be responsive to a world that "might be otherwise" than it was.

> ### *DYNAMIC FOUR*
> *Don't gaze into a mirror.*
> *Look out the windows.*
> *See what might be otherwise.*

DYNAMIC FIVE

Drink from the Same Water,
but with a Different Cup

• • • • • •

Suppose we were able to share meanings freely without a compulsive urge to impose our view or conform to those of others and without distortion and self-deception. Would this not constitute a real revolution in culture?

DAVID BOHM

• • • • • •

For more than three-quarters of a century, Ruth Benedict's insights concerning the effect of culture on what one sees and how one behaves have been a rich treasure of knowledge. Her classic book, *Patterns of Culture*, was written in 1934 as a study of three primitive cultures. Though significantly huge strides have been made since in her academic field of cultural anthropology, her keen observations are still respected and referred to in these times. Her perceptions and conclusions from her research are still an important commentary on present times, especially in the new global reality of the world. Benedict's abiding conviction as a pioneering cultural anthropologist is this: There is a power inherent in understanding culture—one's own and that of others—that gives people greater control in enjoying their present and creating their future.

She starts her book with a proverb of the Digger Indians: "In the beginning God gave to every people a cup of clay, and from this cup they drank their life." She uses this proverb at the outset to exemplify and conceptualize the important and essential role that culture plays in every society. Benedict goes on to relate her encounter with a Digger Indian chief who extended the proverb. The chief added that all dipped into the same source of water, "but their cups were different."

She described this chief as a simple and humble man who, with this proverb, brought into focus a perspective that had value for him equal to life itself. For the chief this one image of the unique cup of clay was the wisdom that gave understanding and meaning to the whole fabric of his own life, to his people's customs and standards, and to their shared faith and beliefs. We must grasp the importance of Benedict's growing realization as she reflected on the diversity of this man's lived cultural reality, which is completely different from that of the great majority of our Western civilization. For the Westerner, there is the predominance of one cosmopolitan culture, which socially and psychologically is usually not sensitive to other cultures. But Benedict pointed out that this simple man had straddled both the ancient and modern cultures with which his people were forced to contend. She used the word *incommensurable* to describe the lived reality of this man's existence.

The institutional church talks a great deal about the necessity for Catholics to engage and interact with the various cultures found on the globe, especially as was promulgated in Vatican II's document, *Gaudium et Spes* (Joy and Hope). However, outside the Westernized world, and even in traditional Western countries where diverse cultures are being successfully assimilated, there is continued and growing resistance to the positions of the church on a variety of issues. The church is perceived as a purveyor of a God who can only be understood in particular and specific cultural, philosophical, theological, and spiritual constructs: all of which are Westernized.

Whether it involves the rubrics of liturgy, dependence on Thomistic philosophy, the role of women, sex and marriage, governance in the church, or myriad other aspects, the institutional church has become rigid in how these situations can be discussed or understood if one is to remain or become a Catholic. It seems that even those in the church's hierarchy who grew up in different cultures can only achieve an exalted position in the church if they have been educated and formed into the correct (from the institution's point of view) way of worshiping and proclaiming the Gospel.

Here, again, is where Catholic schools can serve the entire church. Catholic educators would be well served to visit the principles and ideas of social scientists such as Ruth Benedict when it comes to grasping the impact of diverse cultures on people's perception of themselves and their God. As the Digger Indian proverb highlights, all peoples receive life as they drink from the same well of water, but the God of all creation did not give each person the same cup from which to drink. Culture is a meaning-creation system by which people define themselves, integrate their behavior with that of others, and carry forward their values.

Graduates of every Catholic school, from grade school through graduate education, should know this truth: Each person on Earth is a creature of culture, yet there is no culture that is totally comprehensible, since culture is variable and diverse, neither fixed nor static. All people are dipping their cup into the same water, i.e., the one, God-given reality; but because they have their different cups—their own unique cultures—they see and understand that reality differently and with a variety of perceptions.

• • • • • •

Each person on Earth is a creature of culture, yet there is no culture that is totally comprehensible

• • • • • •

Of course, this truth poses significant and intimidating challenges for societies, nations, and especially religions. Obviously, if we do not want to resort to a relativistic approach in which no truth exists except our own perceptions, then daunting hurdles to dialogue are placed on the road to world harmony and peace by our difference in culture.

In a fascinating book, *Beyond Culture*, Edward T. Hall, a renowned creative anthropologist, emphasizes this situation. Hall contends that, in order to overcome these diverse cultural differences, the differences must first be recognized and made explicit. Then, if the differences are honored and respected on all sides, they may be embraced as a prerequisite to arriving at some universals about human nature. In essence, Hall indicates that people must transcend their own culture. And that is difficult since it is not only a matter solely of transcending the apparent, overt, and obvious cultural traits but also overcoming the more difficult aspects of culture, i.e., the subconscious and less visible culture embedded in people's institutions, including their religious institutions.

Hall goes on further and criticizes the delusory Western cultural conviction that believes it has a monopoly on understanding reality. Explicitly, he terms the West's proclivity to exclusivity as its "pipeline to God." As such, the Western bias has the perspective that other cultures' views are distortions or inferior systems of thought. Being fair, though, Hall points out that is the same problem with other cultures that view their values and beliefs as superior to the West's.

We Catholics must begin to identify our own religious culture in a much more radical way than the specific institutional infrastructure and practices that have evolved over the years. We must be radical in the sense of embracing the spirit of Jesus and his early followers, who saw the Good News as truly for all nations. You did not have to be a Jew, worship as a Jew, or even think like a Jew to be a follower of Jesus. You had only to believe in the Father and respond to the Spirit. You no longer had to follow a prescribed, rigid rubric of formulaic pieties for justification; rather you had to feed the hungry, clothe the poor, and love your neighbor.

This is the dynamic that Catholic schools need to develop. Describing the Catholic Church, James Joyce said it well in *Finnegan's Wake*: "Here comes everybody." Well, this is no longer the reality found in the institutional church. Catholic schools can bring "everybody" back.

This shrinking globe of the third millennium has brought together more diverse cultures than ever before in the history of the world. This compels all, especially the *catholic* (as in "universal") school, to openly study and embrace differences in the basic attitudes of people from various cultures. This necessarily and naturally leads to different approaches to understanding how authority is accepted, how sin is perceived, how God is worshipped, and how life itself is lived. The Catholic Church must be welcoming and open to all. It can do this and remain faithful to the truth of the Gospel of Jesus Christ because the church is not its rules and regulations. The church must always and unambiguously be unafraid to place love of a person—any person—above protection of its authority.

DYNAMIC FIVE
Grasp the impact of culture on people,
including your own on you.
Do not judge; seek to understand.
Place love, not authority, at the center.

DYNAMIC SIX

Uncover and Celebrate
What the Shadows Reveal

• • • • • •

*If you are what you should be,
you will set the whole world ablaze.*

Saint Catherine of Siena

• • • • • •

Several years ago, Roberto Casati, a research director in Paris at the *Centre Nationale de la Reserche Scientifique*, wrote a fascinating book titled *The Shadow Club*. In this work, he studies the cognition of strange things: images, colors, sounds, places, and shadows.

In the opening chapter, Casati discusses the first time he carefully and consistently watched a lunar eclipse. He reflected on the "mechanics" of this phenomenon, i.e., the Earth passes between the sun and the moon. He marveled that, in essence, the shadow created was "our" shadow—yours, mine, and all the rest of the people on Earth—that passed across the moon.

Then, he wondered about the monthly phases of the moon: quarter, half, and full moons. Sometimes, he noted, the quarter moon is on the left, and sometimes on the right. Sometimes there is no moon at all. Casati then observes:

The phases of the moon are illusory changes because they are nothing more than a display of shadow, seen from different points of view as the moon revolves around the Earth. But where does this shadow come from?

It comes from the sun, of course: moon's everlasting source of light. It is the sun, which is the same source of light for our world. The seemingly ever-cyclically changing moon is not changing at all. It is simply a shadow game, and a beautiful one at that. Casati did some thinking that night and came to a transformative conclusion: Shadows do not hide, they reveal!

Since time immemorial, until only a few hundred years ago really, human-kind did not know that the moon got its light from the sun. It was not known that the phases of the moon were simply due to our perspective of that part of the moon that remained unlit because the sun was lighting something else: the Earth.

Shadows do not necessarily hide truth. They reveal truth, since there can only be shadows if there is a source of light to begin with and something to block that light.

For centuries onto millennia, the church has been the source of the "light" responsible for casting revealing shadows all over the Earth, shadows that made the Gospel of Jesus Christ come alive in the lives of people. But it may be fair to at least acknowledge that the traditional brightness of the church's light is fading. It is becoming more difficult to see the truth in the shadows that the cross of Christ casts over the world. Catholic schools can help reverse that trend—if they can identify the source of light and the things that block that light.

In this the third millennium, long since the star lighted the night sky that cast the shadow over the town in Bethlehem, revealing that a Savior was born, there are other light sources casting shadows over the globe. Look at the chart on the following page.

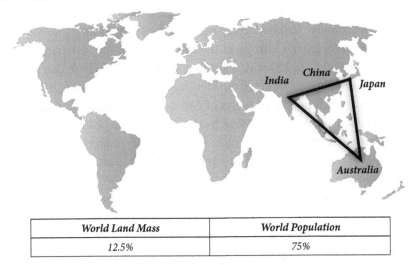

World Land Mass	World Population
12.5%	75%

Draw an imaginary line from a point that begins in India, passes through China, and ends in Japan. Then drop lines from there to form the point of a triangle that is created, with the point touching the top of Australia. That triangle encompasses about 12.5 percent of the landmass on the entire globe. Yet, on that relatively small piece of solid terrain, approximately 75 percent of the entire world's population lives. Also, this area of the world is realizing unprecedented economic growth that has accompanied its religious and geo-political importance.

Now take a closer look at that small triangular landmass and see the incredibly new and big shadow that is being cast on the globe in today's world. This new source of significant light casting its shadow is quite different from the light cast by the Westernized values, traditions, theology, and philosophy of the Roman Catholic Church. For the most part, this 75 percent of the world's population *looks* differently, *thinks* differently, *acts* differently, and *believes* differently than the light source that is emanating today from Rome!

Then, if observers turn their heads from the light source of the triangle, they will see another great and different light source shining out from the African continent. Consider the important research of Philip Jenkins, a professor of history and religious studies, in his book, *The Next Christendom: The Coming of Global Christianity*. Jenkins points out that, by the year 2050, sub-Saharan Africa will have surpassed Europe as the leading center of Christianity. In addition, there are other light sources shining forth over the globe that are quite different from the one in Rome. Consider that Brazil, Mexico, the Philippines, Nigeria, Congo, and the United States of America will have more than 600 million Christians. However, emanating from these sources of light will be shadows cast that are startlingly different and opposing revelations of Christianity.

Jenkins' research clearly demonstrates that the greatest wave of future Christian growth in these parts of the world will not be with Catholic or mainstream Christian sects. The growth will come predominantly from Pentecostals. Born in the early 20th century, Pentecostalism emphasizes personal faith, biblical literalism, and apocalyptic visions. None of this resembles the Christianity of the traditional Catholic Church's teachings; yet it is that very different light source that will be casting a growing shadow over global Christianity.

Now, consider the research of Bernard Lewis in his book, *The Crisis of Islam: Holy War and Unholy Terror*. Lewis' research has shed considerable light on the current understanding of the Muslim world. He uses historiography, jurisprudence, and culture in Islamic society in the Middle East to describe Islam's theological basis for *jihad* and martyrdom. Despite one's political viewpoint, if one studies Lewis' work, the conclusion will be that terrorism and the desire to fight infidels and apostates do not have a convincing or supportable basis in Islamic scripture. Actually, terrorism runs counter to centuries of Islamic tradition; yet Islamic fundamentalists now cast a shadow on the entire globe that runs counter to a peaceful tradition. If some of these negative shadows persist in the world, the lights from which they emanate will necessarily continue to diminish the Christian tradition of peace on Earth and good will to *all* (not just the *many*).

Jenkins predicts that by 2050 almost 20 of the 25 largest nations will be predominantly or entirely Christian or Muslim, with at least ten of those nations being sites of intense conflict. In fact, Jenkins believes that such near-term conflict will make the bloody religious wars of the 16th century look like calisthenics.

We must be humble enough to understand and appreciate that other people, cultures, and religions also have much to contribute to casting shadows on the Earth.

• • • • • •

These observations of the significantly changing landscape of the globe could have either a life-saving or a life-threatening effect on the church. Closely allied to Dynamic 5, in which differences are overcome only when there is understanding, Dynamic 6 for Catholic schools insists we Catholic educators must adapt our language and way of describing the overlapping shadows in a globalized world so that our students can do the same.

To adapt does not mean that we have to negate the truth of the Gospel. It does mean, though, that we must be humble enough to understand and appreciate that other people, cultures, and religions also have much to contribute to casting shadows on the Earth. In fact, these other religions and belief systems are now casting their shadows over more of the globe than the Catholic Church does. As John Micklethwait and Adrian Wooldridge said in their book, *God is Back*:

> The triumph of pluralism means that all religious beliefs (and indeed all secular beliefs) become competitors in the market place. Much though some countries struggle against it, globalization is throwing different religions together.

And, no matter how fond the institutional church is of saying that the church is the *fullness* of the truth and the faith, it must also come to appreciate that this should not mean that it is the *only* valid expression of truth and faith. If we Catholic educators continue to hold on to our own culturally biased ways and forms of speaking of Jesus and his church, we will only help diminish the source of the light that Catholicism has been for the past two millennia.

Some very important facts that the Micklethwait and Wooldridge research brought to light demonstrate the necessity for Catholic schools to transform their current mind-set and culturally biased ways. For instance:

- By 2050, China might be both the world's largest Muslim nation *and* its biggest Christian nation.
- The core of Christianity today in China is urban and Protestant, with women as the predominant evangelizers.
- A 2006 Russian poll showed that 84 percent of the Russian population believed in God.
- There are now 24 million Pentecostal Christians in Brazil and 5.7 million in the USA, and those numbers are growing. It is the fastest growing world religious movement, and currently amounts to 25 percent of the world's Christian population, compared to just 6 percent thirty years ago.
- In South Korea, David Cho's Yoido Full Gospel Church has five of the world's ten biggest megachurches, with 830,000 total members, with that number rising by 3,000 a month.

Now look at some other statistics that Micklethwait and Wooldridge research have uncovered regarding the Western world. For instance:

- Ten percent of Americans are ex-Catholic.
- Those who have left Catholicism outnumber those who have joined the Catholic Church by a margin of nearly 4 to 1.
- In Great Britain, two-thirds of those 18 to 24 described themselves as non-religious, and over half of those did not even believe Jesus of Nazareth existed as a historical figure.
- Only 1 in 10 people in France say God plays an important role in their lives. (That percentage is 90 percent in Muslim countries.)
- In 2004, only one priest was ordained in Dublin. Dublin!

It certainly appears that those in the church's hierarchy who say that they prefer a smaller but more "orthodox" Catholic Church are certainly getting their wish! However, that is not the message proclaimed by Jesus Christ, who came to this world to save the entire world—not just a particular culture in the world or only people who are willing to ignore all the other shadows they see.

DYNAMIC SIX
Illuminate the beauty of religious variety
in the world for all to see.
Help uncover the truths each shadow reveals.
Do not pretend there is but one shadow over the world.

DYNAMIC SEVEN

Nurture Nature Naturally

• • • • • •

There is no good trying to be more spiritual than God. God never meant man to be purely a spiritual creature. That is why He uses material things like bread and wine to put new life into us. We may think this rather crude and unspiritual. God does not. He invented eating. He likes matter. He invented it.

C.S. Lewis

• • • • • •

Most religious people perceive God's grace in their lives as a *natural* intervention, made possible by the all-loving Creator. Grace makes it possible for believers to lead moral lives of faith. A more secular viewpoint emphasizes the *nurturing* aspects of grace within a cultural environment that promotes ethical behavior and respect for others. Actually, moral and ethical practices foster good behavior as a natural consequence of life lived properly, whether one prefers a divine or a secular explanation. Or, as the 20th century British philosopher Antony Flew would keenly point out, "Is conduct right because the gods command it? Or, do the gods command it because it is right?"

Michael Gazzaniga, professor of psychology and director of the Sage Center for the Study of the Mind at Santa Barbara's University of California, has devoted much of his research to investigating how the brain enables the mind and the implications of that process for human ethical behavior. In his intriguing book *The Ethical Brain*, he leaves his familiar field of neuroscience and tackles the study of neuroethics: how people make moral and ethical judgments.

He emphasizes that—although the *brain* is an automatic, rule-driven organ—a *person* is a responsible agent, not an automaton that reacts in uniform ways to common sets of stimuli. Gazzaniga is convinced that each person's brain has a faculty for adapting to what is good. Nevertheless, each person is also truly free in his or her choice of action and can therefore choose evil. It is the person who has responsibility to act morally and ethically, not the brain.

Although Gazzaniga is not an ethicist, he exhorts all of us to commit ourselves to the view that a universal human ethic is possible—not in the sense that there is an automatic drive in our brain that makes us be ethical but in the sense that through our own responsible acts we can choose to do ethics.

Catholic schools can be centers of human ethics, but only if we learn to nurture nature naturally. Whether we accept Gazzaniga's conclusions, or credit God's grace, or emphasize the role of nurture, there is a meaningful commonality in the search for an ethical standard: All these positions, in some way, incorporate Natural Law principles. That is, they all share an understanding that universal truths, moral behavior, and ethical actions are rooted in human nature and can be known through human reason. Natural Law, from an anthropological view, is seeing reality in terms of human experience and values, and has been the predominant paradigm for centuries.

Is this still the case in the world today? Is nature still "natural"?

The natural world has always consisted of time and space. Space has been understood as the infinite extension of a three-dimensional geography in which all matter exists. Christians, especially, have understood time, as that finite duration that belongs to the material universe, as distinct from God's eternity, which has no beginning and no end.

However, in the world today there has been an evolution in the understanding of what has been considered the most basic natural truth expressed in the traditional concepts of time and space. Coined by science fiction writer William Gibson in a 1982 short story, the word *cyberspace* has now become common usage. Instead of the traditional understanding of time and space, cyberspace created a new, virtual reality. This virtual reality does not exist in a physical place; rather it exists in the realm of electronic space. (Whatever and wherever that is!)

In virtual reality, objects are no longer measured as entities in time and space; rather they exist as virtual objects in imaginary places. Thus young people playing their virtual-reality games are able to operate, move, and create a different kind of reality, unencumbered by the natural restrictions of time and space.

To define this new (unnatural?) space, a word was introduced to describe the phenomenon: *eidetic*. Eidetic imagery is a metaphoric location in which persons can vividly experience their or others' visual imagery or creations.

This new phenomenon of cyberspace, which certainly changed what is considered natural, now affects the world's economies, social order, communications, literature, culture, and news. Can anyone doubt that it has not also affected religion, and seemingly affected it more than any other area of life in the globalized world of the third millennium?

Any Catholic school that does not understand this phenomenon and take it into account in its pedagogical program is doomed to failure. After all, with the introduction of cyberspace, and its revolutionary effect in all areas of society, people are given a new freedom that was never as pervasive in a world restricted by natural space and time. This new (different from anything natural?) dimension opens the realm of human imagination to delve into and explore mystery as never before. And since religion, in the "spiritual geography" of the modern world, embraces mystery in this new dimension, it necessarily opens new vistas and horizons never before imagined.

Cyberspace opens the realm of human imagination to delve into and explore mystery as never before.

In cyberspace jargon, a *matrix* is something that constitutes the place or point from which something else originates, takes form, and develops. In this new way for the imagination of the modern person to see mystery, the Ultimate Matrix is God! Can there be any doubt that all religions, especially Christianity, must reckon with the imagination that seeks the mystery of God in new ways that don't rely on traditional dictums, dogma, and doctrines?

Is nature still natural? Well, certainly, not any longer in the world of cyberspace. For Catholic schools not to embrace the emergence of this new paradigm is to doom its future, effectiveness, and relevance.

However, cyberspace is not the only area in the modern world that is tampering with the traditional understanding of what is natural. On May 21, 2010, an online *Wall Street Journal* article by Robert Lee Hotz appeared. Titled "Scientists Create Synthetic Organism," it reported the creation of a synthetic cell completely controlled by man-made genetic instructions. Richard Ebright at Rutgers University, who was not involved with the project, said, "This is literally a turning point in the relationship between man and nature. For the first time, someone has generated an entire artificial cell with predetermined properties."

All of us humans have conditioned our worldview on the accepted fact that the real world is composed of natural systems. Whether we believe in evolution or in intelligent design or in pure chance, up until now we all believed that nature evolved naturally in natural time and space!

But now the world is confronted with a developing synthetic biology, a synthetic evolution, and probably in the near future some version of a synthetic person. Not only is there now the actual creation of a synthetic cell, but there is cloning, DNA manipulation, and mapping of the human genome. There are bio-chemical mind-altering drugs that change human emotions, behaviors, and appetites of all kinds.

How does free will develop in such an "unnatural" world? No longer are we in the *anthropological* world, where we had the "natural" law to guide us. Today there is developing an *anthropogenic* world of synthetic evolution. This is a world qualitatively different from anything we humans have experienced in the past. This is a world where not only scientists and governments but also those of us in the religion business have to ask, "Where will free will and natural law principles be a few decades from now?" Catholic schools should be on the forefront of that question.

Humans more and more *can* and *will* choose *who* and *what* they will become. That is why the Catholic school needs to transform itself so it can respond to this emerging new world. In order to respond to the "signs of the times" (as Vatican II called them) Catholic educators must understand that past solutions are present failures. Reality is not changing. It has already changed. The church, with the unencumbered assistance of Catholic schools, must be responsive to the unfolding epiphany before it is too late.

It may help us to recall the words of poet Elizabeth Barrett Browning:

Earth's crammed with heaven
and every common bush afire with God
but only he who sees
takes off his shoes;
the rest sit round it
and pluck blackberries.

> **DYNAMIC SEVEN**
> *Embrace cyberspace and use it to teach mystery.*
> *Update natural law to include the unnatural.*
> *Be responsive to the unfolding epiphany.*

DYNAMIC EIGHT

Go Faster

• • • • • •

Both the Trinity and quantum mechanics, subatomic physics are different ways of talking in quasi-metaphorical language about what is going on in a system that isn't reducible to facts in the way we normally think of facts.

KATHRINE JEFFERTS SCHORI
(Presiding Bishop of the Episcopal Church)

• • • • • •

On January 31, 2007, Pope Benedict XVI proved that not only can simple things be complicated but also that they may become much more than complicated. He was speaking to a general audience in the Vatican's Audience Hall, talking about the church's early times. At a certain point in his presentation he set aside his text to drive home a point. "The apostles and the first disciples weren't perfect," he said, "but had their own arguments and controversies."

"This appears very consoling to me," the Pope said, "because we see that the saints did not drop as saints from heaven. They were men and women like us with problems and even sins."

The audience of about 6,000 applauded enthusiastically, more so than might be expected. With that, the Pope paused, looked up surprisingly and smiled awkwardly. It seemed that the audience responded very positively to Pope Benedict's simple suggestion that saints could also be sinners. Of course, as we can easily understand, journalists in attendance were then eager to review the official transcript of his remarks.

When the text was released a few hours later, it looked somewhat different than they had heard it. Gone was the line about the sins of the saints. Instead, the official version quoted the Pope as saying that the early saints "were men like us with problems that were complicated."

So the institutional church took the real words of the pope and changed them from saying even the saints lead lives that were in some ways sinful, like all people, to saying they had lives that had problems that were complicated. The Pope at this audience had spoken in Italian and the official Vatican explanation for the confusion was that the Pope had said *complicati*, which translates as "complicated." They said that the listeners were mistaken and that it only sounded as if the Pope said *con peccati*, which means "with sins."

The reader may wish to know that, after the journalists listened carefully to a recording of the Pope's comments, there was no doubt that he actually said "with sins," i.e., *con peccati*.

When Pope Benedict XVI spoke for that brief moment from his heart and not from his prepared script, it really resonated with the people and opened their hearts in a spontaneous display of appreciation for his good, Christian, common sense. If only the institutional church had approached its recent complicated scandals and openly professed its sinfulness from the start, perhaps it would not be in the quandary it is in today. Instead, apparently, the institutional church did not have enough faith that the People of God would forgive them their sins!

• • • • • •

Instead of esoteric theological explanations or pietistic exhortations, the Pope spoke to them, the People of God, about the real world.

• • • • • •

Actually it really didn't matter whether the Pope was underscoring the complicated or sinful nature of holiness in people or the church. The point that people appreciated was that instead of esoteric theological explanations or pietistic exhortations, the Pope spoke to them, the People of God, about the real world, in which every problem is complicated and every person is sinful.

Throughout this book, the focal point has been to center on the necessity for Catholic schools to create new ways of harnessing the power of the Gospel in a globalized world that is quantitatively and qualitatively different from the time Jesus walked on this Earth. Imagination that will see ways to communicate with a diverse and pluralistic world reality is essential now. It is clear that old-fashioned ways, with reliance on Westernized ways of theologizing, philosophizing, and evangelizing, will not bring people beyond the story of Christ's Gospel in the third millennium.

Of course, this type of radical change is never easy for any institution, but it is especially difficult for the institutional church, which has relied on control and equates "orthodox" ways of thinking, talking, and operating with truth. Perhaps it would be appropriate for Catholic educators to remind the institutional church of the words of famous race car driver Mario Andretti: "If everything is under control you're probably not going fast enough!"

Not to be in control, in a traditional sense, is necessary in the incredibly fast pace of communication that exists today. Learning, understanding, and believing no longer take place only in the traditional Western sense of rational, direct, dualistic, linear, and controlled approaches. Some have introduced the word circumambulation to explain this evolving chaotic process. Circumambulation involves a process that looks at reality in a pluralistic world from different sides and many levels of reality. As Nietzsche aptly observed, "You need chaos in your soul to give birth to a dancing star." And if there is one thing that Catholic schools should be doing, it is giving birth to dancing stars: our students.

An emphasis on energizing new imagination in Catholic schools would help us construct new visions, capacities, meaningfulness, and metaphors to help Christianity in general and Catholicism in particular develop the insights to anticipate the transformation needed in the church today. In this regard G.K. Chesterton in his book *Orthodoxy*, keenly observed:

Imagination does not breed insanity. Exactly what does breed insanity is reason. Poets do not go mad; but chess-players do. Mathematicians go mad, and cashiers; but creative artists very seldom. I am not, as will be seen, in any sense attacking logic: I only say that this danger does lie in logic, not in imagination.

Catholic schools must be ready to harness all the imaginative powers of the People of God in order to help the church unfold contemporary progress that has been made in science, genetics, psychology, and human sexuality, as well as spiritual knowledge. This is not to say that traditional moral precepts are no longer true; but neither does it mean that there can be no further enhancement and development in them based on new, verifiable knowledge. Censorship, control, and limiting access to information have been undermined by the Internet. No one (and no institution) can control what people think or what people can discuss and question. And that includes Catholic schools.

I am reminded of Clare Booth Luce's observation that, "Anyone who is not thoroughly confused is not thinking straight." Indeed, this third millennium is probably *con peccati,* just as it was in the past; however, this is also among the most *complicati* times in the history of the world, as well as the church. Complications and sinfulness are not new to the world or to the church. Remember: "God did not send the Son into the world to condemn the world, but that the world might be saved through him" (John 3:17).

Over the centuries, the church has remained faithful to the Gospel of Jesus Christ, not because of its hierarchy or any particular persons; rather, the truth and holiness of the church is real because of the continuous presence of the Holy Spirit in the hearts and minds of the People of God, all of whom—saints included—are sinful and in need of God's healing grace. Cardinal John Henry Newman, an important 19th century English prelate who was beatified in 2010 (a step before possible sainthood), offered this insight in a sermon he gave on March 22, 1829: "O that God would grant the clergy to feel their weakness as sinful men, and the people to sympathize with them and love them and pray for their increase in all good gifts of grace."

Newman's words are as important for the institutional church today as they were in the 19th century or at any time. As I finish this book, Pope Francis, a Jesuit with an advanced degree in science, has just been elected. Perhaps he has been sent by the Holy Spirit to lead us into the new millennium, and perhaps the Catholic schools will stand ready to help him do so. In doing so, we should all heed the advice of St. Augustine: "If you think you have grasped God, it is not God you have grasped."

DYNAMIC EIGHT
Everyone is sinful.
Everything is complicated.
If everything is under control,
you are probably not going fast enough.

CONCLUSION

• • • • • •

*Dear Brothers, Shepherds of God's Holy People, it is of the utmost impor-
tance that openness, honesty and transparency should always be the hallmark of everything that the Church does, in all her spiritual, educational
and social undertakings, as well as in every aspect of her administration.*

POPE JOHN PAUL II

• • • • • •

I truly believe it is the Catholic school that can lead our institutional church
out of its present quandary, take the People of God beyond our present story,
and lead both our church and our world to a glorious transformation into what
Jesus of Nazareth called the kingdom of God, "on earth as it is in heaven." Our
job is nothing less than "to renew the face of the earth" with the love that Jesus
proclaimed for all people in all ages. If we don't do this, we will be "flying in the
face of tradition," as I titled my companion book to this one.

Jesus did not go to the temple religious leaders, but rather called as his
apostles and disciples fishermen, tax collectors, homemakers, ordinary labor-
ers, and all who wanted to join him in helping bring about his vision of the
world as it should and could be. Jesus clearly understood that the lived experience of himself and his followers was a living, changing, developing source of
revelation about the nature of God and what God wants from us. Jaroslav Jan
Pelikan, in *The Vindication of Tradition*, demonstrates how we could explain
Jesus' understanding of tradition:

> Tradition is the living faith of the dead. Traditionalism is the dead faith
> of the living. And, I suppose I should add, it is traditionalism that gives
> tradition such a bad name.

If we Catholic educators embrace tradition rather than traditionalism, we can and will be an effective and powerful force in aiding the institutional church to relate to the faithful and the world writ-large. As Saint Augustine tells us:

Believers are also thinkers; in believing they think, and in thinking they also believe…. If faith does not think, it is nothing.

The world has changed and so too must Catholic education. To change does not mean that the truth of God's revelation has changed. It does mean that we must grow in Christ's love in response to the times. Pope Benedict XVI in 2010 made John Henry Newman "Blessed" on his way to possible sainthood. Perhaps we Catholic educators should heed Cardinal Newman's insight when he said:

In a higher world it is otherwise, but here below to live is to change, and to be perfect is to have changed often.

Catholic educators in Catholic schools and universities around the world are incredibly gifted, loyal, and dedicated women and men who have over many years been true and faithful to the church. They are ready to take their students into the third millennium and in so doing lead the institution church there as well.

Our Catholic schools and universities must foster intellectual openness, nurture spiritual discovery, and model Catholic courage and faith. For this to happen, Catholic educators must be encouraged to explore God's creation with academic freedom and integrity unfettered by any authoritarian rigidity. The grace-filled freedom of students' "faith seeking understanding" is not a process that can be controlled. Rather, it is truly an amazing, joy-filled journey through the winding and meandering muses abounding in the beauty of human cultural diversity.

We must let the Catholic school, first and foremost, be an excellent school.

APPENDIX (See Chapter Two)

In this spirit of Pope Benedict's call to profound and ongoing dialogue, the following chart presents how a church is different from a school, and specifically how the Catholic Church differs from the Catholic school. (Of course, as with any chart presenting differences, in the complex society of the real world such distinctions are never this simple and clear-cut.)

The Catholic Church is not the Catholic School

	The Catholic Church	*The Catholic School*
Objective	*Proclaim Gospel*	Assist church in "exploration" of Gospel message
Focus	*Reveal Ultimate Truth of God* A "Teaching" Collegiality of Authority (The Magisterium)	*"Unfold" proximate truth in the world* (varied manifestations of God) A "Learning" Collegiality of Equals (The Academy)
Methodology	*Deduction* Start with a truth and then enunciate an application ⋎ *Doctrine* (a particular principle)	*Induction* Start with experience (scientific) and formulation of an application ⋎ *Hypothesis* (a proposition/assumption, i.e., a way of interpreting the world in the light of faith)
Duty	*To present divinely inspired truth dogma* (a system of principles that are established)	*To faithfully and accurately explain these doctrines and dogma*
Authenticity	*Faith* Divinely inspired truth	*Reason* Humanly relational, interactive and explorative
Process	*Mystery* resoluteness hierarchical categorical	*Facts* explorative democratic conditional
Goal	*To tell the story* (values the authentic traditions)	*To go beyond the story* (values the richness of diversity)
End	*Certainty*	*Ambiguity*

An explanation of this chart may help us to more clearly understand how the Catholic school is Catholic even though it operates distinctly differently from the Catholic Church. Also, when these areas of distinction are grasped, it becomes easier to see where and how tensions can, do, and indeed should happen if the church is doing its job and the school is permitted to do its job. If each respects the other's role and understands the other's *modus operandi*, then those tensions will be constructive. Also, if each respects the other's role, there is a better chance for the institutional church to unravel the quandary that has arisen from the significant criticism by faithful Catholics and from the general worldwide public that has focused on the hierarchy and the institutional church as a whole.

However, there is much destructive tension currently existing between the church and the school because many in the hierarchy want the Catholic school under the control of the church, at which point this distinction disappears and the Catholic school become just like the Catholic church and ceases to be a school in any meaningful sense.

These are some of the areas that demonstrate the differences that should be respected relative to how the church does its job and how the Catholic school must do its job:

Objective

Among many important ingredients that are part of the mission of the church, probably the most striking is its sacred obligation to proclaim the Gospel. It is the church that has the divinely inspired mandate to present the Good News that Jesus Christ proclaimed. It is the church that is vested with the ultimate authority as the worldly protector of the "deposit of faith" that follows from its teachings and traditions. No other institution has this ultimate authority.

The Catholic school, then, is not the competent "authority" as the "proclaimer" of the Gospel. That sacred duty rests with the church alone. Rather, the Catholic school assists the church through its teaching and research to explore the meaning of that message found in the Gospel. It involves the knowledge, information, and science found in the rational and empirically verifiable world as seen through the lens of culture and society. The church often says in many ways that the transcendent faith of the church always seeks worldly understanding. That is the arena where the Catholic school operates.

And this is where the Catholic school must fulfill its primary role to unfold the sacred and divine mysteries of the faith, even though they can never be fully comprehended in the scientific, secular world of everyday life. In essence, the church is dealing with knowledge that has been given to the faith through divine inspiration; yet the Catholic school is exploring that very message in a world of limited, scientific knowledge, which is by nature necessarily filled with questions, diversity, and doubts.

If the Catholic school does not teach the true Catholic faith as proclaimed by the church in the context of scientific and worldly conditional knowledge, then it is not really a "school." Therefore, constitutive to the Catholic school are exploration, research, questioning, and doubt. This does not make the Catholic school disloyal or even unresponsive to the church; rather, it makes Catholic educators good and loyal "explorers" with the church in helping students freely question their faith in order to seek better understanding. Academic freedom to inquire, to question, and to explore truth cannot be limited in a Catholic school. It cannot have certain questions "off-limits." It cannot restrict interaction with culture and society.

The Catholic Church believes it is founded by Christ to proclaim the truth of the Gospel and that it cannot err in teaching about faith and morals because of the presence of the Holy Spirit. This certainty alone should make the institutional church and its hierarchy the greatest supporters and encouragers of Catholic education to be school, with the freedom and autonomy to do its job. They have literally nothing to fear.

Focus

The focus of the church should be to reveal the ultimate truth of God's existence and nature as revealed in Scripture and Tradition. In doing this the institutional church has developed its understanding of itself as a source of certainty for the People of God. This reality is seen through a teaching collegiality of authority that is called the magisterium of the church.

However, the Catholic school does not have within its mission or purview the revelation of ultimate truths. Unlike the church as a "teaching collegiality of authority," the Catholic school is a "learning collegiality of equals." Instead of a magisterium with final authority as in the church, there is the "academy"—the faculties, teachers, researchers, and other academic personnel—in which nothing is absolute and everything is open to study.

The academy is always interacting within a milieu of conditional information and interacting with culture and society. So, for example, a Catholic school can explain the church's deposit of faith regarding ultimate truth, but it must do so in a continuous and open dialogue with the ever-changing scientific and cultural exigencies extant. Therefore, the focus of the Catholic school is necessarily very different from that of the church. As paradoxical as it may first sound, the Catholic school is loyal and faithful to the church to the degree that it questions, searches, and dialogues with the church in order to be able to make the church's teachings meaningful and consistent with verifiable scientific knowledge and information for its students and society.

Methodology
It should come as no surprise, given the objective and focus of the church, that the methodology it most generally utilizes in arriving at its teachings is through deduction. In other words, the church starts with the revealed truth it already possesses and from that enunciates an application. In this way, as long as it is consistent and logical in deducing from a universal truth, the church can and does present a particular dogma or doctrine applicable to real-life situations.

This is not the methodology that is the predominant paradigm in a learning institution. For a school, the methodology that is mostly utilized is that of induction. As such, in the academy, the researchers and learners start with experience (specifics, particulars) and from that formulate an application. This is often posited as a proposition or hypothesis, i.e., the scientific methodology.

Therefore, within the utilization of these two distinctive ways of arriving at the truth, there is much room for misunderstanding and suspicion. However, the truth is the truth, isn't it? Each methodology will necessarily demonstrate the one, same truth, unless one methodology is deficient in some manner. The church should not fear the scientific methodology presenting something contrary to its teachings, if it has arrived at its dogma or doctrine correctly. In fact, the church should encourage the scientific methodology as a corroboration of its doctrine. Of course, this is not always what happens, and as Shakespeare would say, "There's the rub."

When Galileo demonstrated that the Earth was the center of the universe, should not the church have been edified that he had proved the institutional church to be wrong in what it currently taught? In like manner, should not the church today be less resistive to the current research regarding human sexuality coming from theologians and psychologists? The evolving factual data could be an enormous help to the church in addressing some of its current teachings. However, the many official church statements hindering an open discussion about human sexuality is certainly not respecting the inductive methodology of education. In fact, the current hierarchy may be shutting up the Galileos of modern-day human sexuality.

Duty

Clearly, the church has the duty to help the faithful by developing a system of doctrines or dogma, a deposit of faith if you will. An essential way to present the divinely inspired truths is for the institutional church to use its collegial authority as the magisterium to help the People of God understand the revealed truth that Jesus entrusted to the church. The duty to develop this deposit of faith is so important for all that Catholics believe the Holy Spirit guides the church and inspires it in this sacred task.

The Catholic school, on the other hand, is not charged with any duty regarding the church's deposit of faith, except to faithfully and accurately explain these doctrines and dogma to its students. However, this must not be interpreted as a restrictive duty. In other words, it is not contrary to its duty when a Catholic school accurately explains Catholic teaching yet also permits its students the freedom to question and dialogue about that teaching. For example, a Catholic educator is free to teach the Catholic social teaching on the rights of workers to organize unions and bargain collectively yet still have a discussion about whether unions might be corrupt or harmful to the economy.

It is also not contrary to the duty of the Catholic school if, in the academy, there is research or information that is made available to the institutional church so that it may be better able to develop its teachings. Again, recognizing the distinctive duty of church and school does not negate a complementarity that cooperation fosters. In fact, the church and the school should always accept such cooperation so that each can better perform its respective duty to seek the truth.

Authenticity

Since it is the church that has the duty to present its divinely inspired truth, obviously there is not a human approach that can verify what is a matter of faith. Normal and expected rational activities cannot always be followed in such circumstances when trying to establish validity in this realm. It does not mean that divinely inspired truths are irrational; rather they are *supra-rational*, i.e., beyond the scope of reason. For instance, no amount of rational machinations or systematic application of logic will ever give rise to the truth that God is One and is also Three Divine Persons. Yet most of the faithful believe and accept this truth even though it is beyond the power of reason alone to discover this relative to the degree of faith that they have in the church's authenticity in revealing the mysteries of God.

There is no corresponding legitimacy and validity in a Catholic school that empowers such divinely inspired authenticity. The authenticity of that faith, as taught by the church's magisterium, is not in the realm of the school. The Catholic school, through reason, interacts with its students to explore and situate the faith as beyond the domain of rational discovery. Authenticity for the Catholic school lies in the human relational interactions of explaining, dialoguing, testing, and exploring divinely inspired truths as taught by the church.

Process

In the unique attributes within this process of authenticity there is much room for misunderstanding and the occasion for tense clashes between the institutional church and the Catholic school. The process for the institutional church in teaching the faith embraces mystery—not teaching, for example, a chemical or mathematical formula for the scientific proof that the Holy Spirit is present among us or in quantifying Christ's love for the sinner.

The process that involves the mystery of faith and its divinely inspired teachings is, necessarily, categorical, hierarchical, and resolute. How else can you process the truth as it is given to you through divine inspiration? That kind of knowledge is not necessarily empirically verifiable. Therefore, authenticity of the faith involves the authority of whoever is presenting the revelation found in Sacred Scripture and Tradition. The faithful, for the most part, believe that authority is vested in the magisterium of the church, even though they may not quite understand how it is exercised.

This is not the case for the Catholic school. The Catholic school is not the authority that determines the revelation found in Sacred Scripture and Tradition. The school is actually part of the *sensus fidelium*, the lived experience of the faithful, obligated to present the faith in ways it can be understood within the culture and society. Mystery and faith are not conducive to purely rational explanations. The process that a Catholic school must utilize in order to be credible is in the use of reason, dialogue, and investigation. The Catholic school helps students to explore and discover the truth, giving them complete freedom to make their own decisions.

The process that the school uses in furthering the Catholic faith is not one of proselytizing; rather, it is democratic and conditional. The church has always taught that faith is a gift from God. Therefore, the Catholic school must open the eyes and the minds of its students to see the divine in all of creation. Again, for the Catholic school to do this, it must have the courage and freedom to explore, without restrictions, all viewpoints and knowledge with its students.

Goal

In examining all these differences, it becomes clear that there are different goals that must be kept in mind by the church and the school. Obviously, in the entire *modus operandi* of the church, all must value the traditions and teachings that have been preserved in the church for over 2,000. Indeed, the church must guard, proclaim, and tell the story of Sacred Scripture: the Word made flesh.

The Catholic school, with all the powers and abilities it has as school, has the goal of going "beyond the story" presented by the church and work closely with its students to bring the world and the Word together so that it might be understood by all. The Catholic school goes beyond the story when it teaches theology and theatre, music and mathematics, philosophy and psychology, and all the arts, humanities, and sciences.

End

So where does the tension exist? In the end, the church is about the certainty that faith has the power with which to gift the believer with salvation. The Catholic school is about the ambiguity that is present when the human mind encounters the mystery of the omnipotence of God.

Thank God for a life of certainty as found in the divinely inspired faith of the church.

And, thank God for a life filled with graced ambiguity as the Catholic school seeks more understanding of that certainty, which understanding sometimes escapes us in the world of pure reason.

SELECTED BIBLIOGRAPHY

Benedict, Ruth. *Patterns of Culture*. New York: Mariner Books, 2006.

Beaudoin, T. *Virtual Faith: The Irreverent Spiritual Quest of Generation X*. Indianapolis: Jossey-Bass, 2000.

Buckley, Michael J., S.J. *The Catholic University as Promise and Project: Reflections in a Jesuit Idiom*. Georgetown: Georgetown University Press, 1998.

Chesterton, G. K. *Orthodoxy*. Garden City: Doubleday, 1936.

Congar, Yves, (trans. John Bowden).*The Meaning of Tradition*. Ignatius.com: Ignatius Press, 2004.

De Thomasis, Louis, and Neal St. Anthony. *Doing Right in a Shrinking World: How Corporate America Can Balance Ethics & Profit in a Changing Economy*. Austin: Greenleaf Bookgroup Press, 2006.

Dulles, Avery. *Models of the Church*. The Doubleday Religious Publishing Group, 1991.

Ellenson, David. "Building a World in Which God Would Be Happy to Live." *Jews and Judaism in the Twenty-First Century: Human Responsibility, the Presence of God, and the Future of Covenant*. ed. Edward Feinstein. Woodstock, VT: Jewish Lights Publishing, 2007.

Ferguson, Marilyn, and John Naisbitt. *The Aquarian Conspiracy: Personal and Social Transformation in Our Time*. Los Angeles: J. P. Tarcher, 1987.

Gallagher, Michael Paul, S.J. *Clashing Symbols*. New York: Paulist Press, 2003.

Gazzaniga, Michael. *The Ethical Brain: The Science of Our Moral Dilemmas*. New York: Harper Perennial, 2006.

Geertz, Clifford. *After the Fact: Two Countries, Four Decades, One Anthropologist*. (Jerusalem Harvard Lectures). Cambridge: Harvard University Press, 1996.

George, Margaret. *Mary Called Magdalene*. New York: Penguin, 2003.

Groome, Thomas H. *Educating for Life: A Spiritual Vision for Every Teacher and Parent*. Allen, TX: The Crossroad Publishing Company, 2001.

Hall, Edward T. *Beyond Culture*. New York: Anchor Books, 1976.

Jenkins, Philip. The Next Christendom: The Coming of Global Christianity, New York: Oxford University Press, USA, 2007.

Johnson, Elizabeth A.,C.S.J. *Truly Our Sister, A Theology of Mary in the Communion of Saints*. Maryknoll, NY: Orbis Books, 2010.

Johnson, Elizabeth A.,C.S.J. *Quest for the Living God*. NY: Continuum, 2007

Kasper, Cardinal Walter. *Theology and the Church*. New York: Crossroad Publishing Company, 1989.

Klein, Eliahu, trans. *Kabbalah of Creation: The Mysticism of Isaac Luria, Founder of Modern Kabbalah*. Northvale, NJ: Jason Aronson, 2000.

Lawler, Michael, and Todd Salzman. *The Sexual Person: Toward a Renewed Catholic Anthropology*. Georgetown: Georgetown University Press, 2008.

Lewis, Bernard. *The Crisis of Islam-Holy War and Unholy Terror*. New York: Random House Trade Paperbacks, 2004.

Mello, Anthony de, S.J. *The Song of the Bird*, Chicago: Loyola University Press, 1983.

Merleau-Ponty, Maurice. *Humanism and Terror*. Boston: Beacon Press, 1969.

Micklethwait, John, and Adrian Woodridge. *God Is Back: How the Global Revival of Faith Is Changing the World*. New York: Penguin Press, 2009.

Miguens, Fernando. *Fe y Cultura en la Ensenanza de Juan Pablo II*. Madrid: Ediciones Palabra, 1994.

Morgan, Gareth. *Images of Organization*. Thousand Oaks, CA: Sage Publications, 2006.

Morrison, Toni. *Beloved*. New York: Alfred A. Knopf, 1987.

Nienhaus, Cyndi A., C.S.A, Ph.D. "Transformation of the World: Covenant-Centric Christian Religious Education" (2008), unpublished. Fordham University, 2008.

O'Murchu, Diarmuid. *Quantum Theology: Spiritual Implications of the New Physics*. New York: The Crossroad Publishing Company, 2004.

Ong, Walter, J., S.J. "Where Are We Now? Some Elemental Cosmological Considerations." *Theology Digest* 48:2, 2001.

Phan, Peter C., ed. James L. Heft. "Religious Identity and Belonging Amidst Diversity and Pluralism: Challenges and Opportunities for the Church and Theology," *Passing on the Faith: Transforming Traditions for the Next Generation of Jews, Christians, and Muslims*. New York: Fordham University Press, 2006.

Pottmeyer, Hermann J. *Towards a Papacy in Communion*. New York: Herder & Herder, 1998.

Robinson, Geoffrey. *Confronting Power and Sex in the Catholic Church*. Sydney: John Garratt Pub.: 2007.

Rohr, Richard. *Things Hidden: Scripture As Spirituality*. Cincinnati: St. Anthony Messenger Press: 2008.

Rohr, Richard, and John Bookser Feister. *Hope Against Darkness: The Transforming Vision of Saint Francis in an Age of Anxiety*. Cincinnati: St Anthony Messenger Press, 2001.

Rush, Osmond. *Still Interpreting Vatican II*. New York: Paulist Press, 2004.

Sacks, Jonathon. *The Dignity of Difference: How to Avoid the Clash of Civilizations*. New York: Continuum, 2003.

Schaefer, Judith K., O.P. *The Evolution of a Vow: Obedience as Decision Making in Communion*. Munich: LitVerlag, 2008.

Schillebeeckx, Edward. *Christ: The Christian Experience in the Modern World*. Canterbury: SCM-Canterbury Press Ltd, 1982.

Schillebeeckx, Edward. *Christ the Sacrament of the Encounter With God*. Lanham, MD: Sheed & Ward, 2007.

Seewald, Peter. *Light of the World: The Pope, the Church, and the Signs of the Times*. San Francisco: Ignatius Press, 2010.

Sheplace, Linda J. *Lifting the Veil: The Feminine Face of Science*. Boston: Shambala, 1993.

Tillard, J. M. R. (trans. Madeleine Beaumont). *Flesh of the Church*. Collegeville: The Liturgical Press, 2001.

BOOKS OF RELATED INTEREST

GREAT AMERICAN CATHOLIC EULOGIES
Compiled and introduced by Carol DeChant
Foreword by Thomas Lynch

Fifty eulogies, printed memorials, and elegiac poems that give a real feel for the "lived experience" of American Catholics from colonial times to the present.

INVITATION TO CATHOLICISM
INVITATION TO THE OLD TESTAMENT
INVITATION TO THE NEW TESTAMENT
Alice Camille

Three companion books by award-winning author Alice Camille that offer clear, concise, and informative explanations of the Catholic understanding of Tradition and Scripture.

CHURCH, CHICAGO-STYLE
William L. Droel
Foreword by Sr. Patricia Crowley, OSB

A celebration of the history of active clerical leadership and lay involvement in the Catholic Church in Chicago over the last fifty years. 126-page paperback, $12.95

SPIRITUALITY AT WORK
THE MASS IS NEVER ENDED
THE WORLD AS IT SHOULD BE
Gregory F. Augustine Pierce

Three books that examine the whats, whys, and hows of the mission of all Christians to help bring about the kingdom of God "on earth, as it is in heaven."

RUNNING INTO THE ARMS OF GOD
THE GEOGRAPHY OF GOD'S MERCY
THE LONG YEARNING'S END
Patrick Hannon, CSC

This trilogy of award-winning stories of the presence of God in daily life by one of the best storytellers in the American Catholic Church.

Available from Booksellers or 800-397-2282
www.actapublications.com